OUR EYES ARE ON YOU

Principles to Prevail in Faith and Prayer

Endorsements

Prayer. Always an imperative. Always a now word. Always a game changer. There is a call of the Spirit going out to the church to return to first things and do what we once understood was essential and non-negotiable. One of those first essential and non-negotiable things is believing, persistent prayer. Many are responding with a fresh cry, "Lord, teach us to pray!" In his book *Our Eyes are On You*, Bob Sawvelle has written a timely and weighty answer to the call and to that cry. This book not only gives a solid foundation to the beginner, but also invites the mature into deeper faith and supernatural adventure. Wherever you find yourself on the prayer spectrum, here is a book to kickstart, renew and perhaps reform your prayer life.

Dr. Kim Maas, International Speaker
Founder/CEO Kim Maas Ministries, Woman of our Time, Ten35Productions
Author of *Prophetic Community: God's Call for All to Minister in His Gifts* (Chosen Books, 2019).

Bob Sawvelle has shown us how to grow in confident faith being assured by the character and purposes of God as they are revealed in the ministry of Jesus and in the pages of His Word. Bob reminds us that a relationship with Jesus is central to our identity and a life of prayer. Strong churches arise from congregations who pray with a certain hope in God's desire to provide good gifts for His sons and daughters that they may impact the world so that the will of God might be done on earth as it is in heaven. *Our Eyes are On You* will provide you with the encouragement and wisdom you need to pray with preserving confidence in the One who has loved you from the beginning.

Dr. Tom Litteer, Assistant Academic Dean at Global Awakening Theological Seminary, Faculty Mentor for Randy Clark Scholars D.Min. Program, United Theological Seminary

Bob and his wife, Carolyn, have ministered in the gifts of the Spirit for decades. Rich with testimonies of breakthrough and perseverance in prayer, this book will increase your faith in God's power and provision. Whether ministering in Haiti, Tucson or around the globe, Bob calls us to a greater expectancy for the miraculous!

Dr. Madeline C. Henners, Director of Contextual Ministries at United Theological Seminary

OUR EYES ARE ON YOU

Principles to Prevail in Faith and Prayer

Bob Sawvelle

Copyright

Unless otherwise indicated, all Scripture is taken from the New King James Version® (NKJV). Copyright © 1982 by Thomas Nelson. Used by permission. All rights reserved.

Scripture quotations taken from the New American Standard Bible® (NASB), Copyright © 1960, 1962, 1963, 1968, 1971, 1972, 1973, 1975, 1977, 1995 by The Lockman Foundation. Used by permission. www.Lockman.org

Scripture quotations taken from the Amplified® Bible (AMPC), Copyright © 1954, 1958, 1962, 1964, 1965, 1987 by The Lockman Foundation. Used by permission. www.Lockman.org

Scripture quotations marked (NLT) are taken from the Holy Bible, New Living Translation, copyright ©1996, 2004, 2015 by Tyndale House Foundation. Used by permission of Tyndale House Publishers, Inc., Carol Stream, Illinois 60188. All rights reserved.

Scripture quotations marked (CEB) are taken from the COMMON ENGLISH BIBLE. © Copyright 2011 COMMON ENGLISH BIBLE. All rights reserved. Used by permission. (www.CommonEnglishBible.com).

Scripture quotations marked (YLT) are taken from the 1898 YOUNG'S LITERAL TRANSLATION OF THE HOLY BIBLE by J.N. Young, (Author of the Young's Analytical Concordance), public domain.

Scripture quotations marked TPT are from The Passion Translation®. Copyright © 2017, 2018 by Passion & Fire Ministries, Inc. Used by permission. All rights reserved. ThePassionTranslation.com.

Our Eyes are On You
Principles to Prevail in Faith and Prayer

Bob Sawvelle
info@passiontucson.org
passiontucson.org
bobsawvelle.com

ISBN: 9798630698292 (paperback)

Copyright © 2020 Bob Sawvelle, all rights reserved.
For more information on how to order this book, contact Bob Sawvelle

Passion Church
1212 South Palo Verde Ave.
Tucson, AZ 85713

Library of Congress Cataloging-in-Publication Data (Pending)

No part of this book may be reproduced, stored or transmitted in any form or by any means, electronic or mechanical, including photocopying and recording, or by any information storage or retrieval system, except as may be expressly permitted in writing by the publisher. Please direct your inquiries to info@passiontucson.org

Dedication

To the faithful ministers and prayer warriors who helped my growth in faith and prayer. To Jim Maher, your life of worship and prayer left a mark—I'm forever grateful. To Rodney Tolleson, your example of faith and courage gave me the confidence to trust God in every situation. To Dick Joyce, your teachings on prayer made an impact and helped set the tone for this book. To Darlene Maisano, thank you for demonstrating confident faith and consistent prayer—God has moved mountains in your behalf! To Randy Clark, your faith for healing ministry, missions, and training the body of Christ has fueled me. To Carolyn, who has never wavered; your life of faith and prayer inspire me—always! To the faithful intercessors at Passion Church, thank you; your commitment to prayer is unwavering—keep praying, mountains are moving!

Table of Contents

Foreword		xi
Introduction		xv
Chapter One	Faith Versus Fear	1
Chapter Two	Help My Unbelief	19
Chapter Three	Expectant Faith	35
Chapter Four	Faith from God	49
Chapter Five	Characteristics of Faith	59
Chapter Six	Prevailing Faith & Prayer	85
Chapter Seven	Lord, Teach Us to Pray	105
Chapter Eight	Do You Have the Right to Ask?	129
Chapter Nine	Elijah's Prayer Principles	147
Chapter Ten	Our Eyes are On You	173
Acknowledgements		197
About the Author		199
Endnotes		201

Foreword

It is one thing to bow a knee and confess that Jesus Christ is Lord. A deeper level of faith is required, however, to walk in victory along a narrow path filled with storms and temptations.

I am confronted daily to consider my faith fuel gauge. My flesh boasts of one who is full of faith and running the race to win. My cup runs over with faith to tackle business issues, relationship vibrations, and various other stumbled-upon opportunities. My heart longs to propel me by faith through the greatest delights and deepest sorrows of life. My hope-well brims with the desire to remain confident in my Father's guiding hand.

Too often, I face those daily moments in which I gaze with amazement at my fuel gauge, which taunts me with an empty faith-light. As my knees buckle with a keen awareness of my waning faith, I quickly remember the father of the boy with an unclean spirit. This man brought his son to the disciples, whose efforts produced nothing. He then approached Jesus, who challenged his faith, *"If you can believe; all things are possible to him who believes"* (Mark 9:23).

The troubled father immediately cried out to Jesus, *"Lord, I believe. Help my unbelief!"* (Mark 9:24b).

We all pass through the valley of unbelief; the cause of our faith-drain varies by circumstances and past experiences. We have learned to look to the Lord when everything around us devolves through the deep entropic process set in motion by the fall. Our eyes lift to our loving God, "Help me, Father."

We cry with waning faith, knowing in our inner knower that God hears our cries. At this moment of rising despair, nothing makes sense in the flesh, yet everything is clear in the spirit. God is working it out.

Our brilliant star of faith shines brightest when we look to the giver of light. The distance from the horizon to the heavens is bridged by the simple faith required to tilt our head with quiet confidence.

As you turn the pages of *Our Eyes are On You* by Pastor Bob Sawvelle, I believe you will pause often to make such a tilt. Your heart will cry out as your knowing stimulates faith-filled awe.

Your journey through my friend's wise words will be filled with many such moments to pause and reflect. Praise and bask in His presence. Keep your journal and pencil at hand. Try to capture what you feel as you read about the wonders of how God blesses your path. Keep your Bible nearby and read Scripture alongside the pages of this book.

Don't be in a hurry to finish this nourishing buffet. Taste and see that the Lord is good. Lift your eyes.

Dr. Steve Greene

Publisher and executive vice president of the multimedia group at Charisma Media and executive producer of the Charisma Podcast Network. His Charisma House book, *Love Leads*, shows that without love, you cannot be an effective leader. Download his Greenelines podcast at *cpnshows.com*.

Lake Mary, Florida

Introduction

As I finish this manuscript, the world is riveted by the COVID-19 pandemic. The global situation is severe, and world leaders are struggling to stop the virus and overcome its health and economic impacts. I started this book a year ago, compelled to help the body of Christ build faith and confidence in prayer; little did I know what was looming on the horizon. This COVID-19 storm is serious, but as we pray and act, it will be stopped.

Prayer elevates our life in Christ beyond the temporal. In prayer, we discover new depths of relationship with our Savior—for prayer is communion. Effective prayer is fueled by resolute faith. His faith, alive within, empowers prayer. It's a faith that sees through the darkness, because it sees Him. Faith that is anchored in Jesus and His Word is a faith that prays until mountains move.

Mature faith creates confident prayer—prayer that gets answers. In response to the disciple's question, *"Lord teach us to pray,"* Jesus responded, *"When you pray…"* and began to give principles how to pray effectively. Throughout God's Word, we are invited to learn how to grow in faith and prevail in prayer.

Faith that moves mountains and sees obstacles overcome is a faith that deepens through ongoing encounter and relationship with Jesus. Jesus is the source of our life and faith—He is the originator and perfecter of our faith. Confident faith is to know Jesus well enough to know His leading through life's circumstances. When, like Jesus, we can see what the Father is doing in every situation, confidence and faith soar.

Faith also develops through God's Word, for *"faith comes by hearing, and hearing by the word of God."* (Rom. 10:17) Both the written Word (*logos*) and Spirit-inspired word (*rhema*) build confidence in the heart to believe what God is promising. The Word of God can create compelling faith, a faith that is never deterred, and never gives up. Prevailing prayer originates with those who are confident in God's Word and revealed will. Faith generates effective prayer.

The essence of prayer is communion with God, grounded in His Word. A Christian life cannot thrive without an ongoing love relationship with the Father through Jesus. To miss the importance of relationship is ineffective at best and borders on using God selfishly. The dynamic life flow of the Spirit, available to a believer through Christ, enables persevering faith and prayer. After all, Jesus stated plainly in John 15 that He was the vine and we are the branches—we are to remain in Him for fruitfulness and the divine flow of life, which only He can give through the indwelling of the Holy Spirit.

There is no quick formula to becoming a person of great faith and prayer. However, God's Word contains principles which will position you to grow in prevailing faith and prayer. Jesus promised, *"ask, and it shall be given you,"* which means He intends for you and me to be confident in the asking. Jesus invites us to journey with Him into a life of audacious faith, believing for the impossible, and impacting our world through prayer.

Our Eyes are On You will provide you important principles from God's Word, personal stories, and the testimony of others to empower your faith and confidence in prayer. God's love and power make a difference. Growing in faith and prayer will impact your life and the world around you. God desires all His people to prevail in faith and prayer, and our world needs a confident, praying Church in this hour.

Chapter One

Faith Versus Fear

"Why are you so fearful? How is it that you have no faith?" Mark 4:40–41

"Not only in prayer, but in duty, the man who has great faith in God, and whom God has girded with strength, how gigantic does he become!" Charles Spurgeon

One of the most repeated commands in Scripture is, "Fear not!" Why? To refuse fear permits faith to flourish. Confident faith is free of fear and full of God's peace during the storms of life.

Everyone has trials and hardships. Your union with Jesus in His death, resurrection, and ascension glory imparts His authority over the chaos of this world and the circumstances you face. Resting in Christ's finished work positions you to live as an overcomer. As a follower of Jesus, you are an heir of God and joint heir with Christ, which affords you His favor, resource, and the power of God's kingdom in this present life.

Many in the body of Christ struggle with fear. For some, it may be a stronghold of fear—perhaps caused by the trauma of past or present events. Have you noticed that there is no shortage of "bad news" in our world? Negative news breeds fear unless one's heart is grounded in Jesus. Jesus taught and demonstrated to the disciples and the crowds the superiority of faith verses fear.

Jesus Calms a Stormy Sea

Our story begins as Jesus and the disciples are leaving the western shore of the Galilee immediately following the conclusion of the seed parables (Mark 4:35–41).

> ...*Let us cross over to the other side...and a great windstorm arose, and the waves beat into the boat, so that it was already filling.* (Mark 4:35–37)

It is God's will and initiative for Jesus and the disciples to get to the other side to free the oppressed and heal the sick. The storm is filling the boat with water—the situation looks dire and the disciples, many who were fishermen, knew the danger of the Sea of Galilee. The storm arises and the men seem powerless to do anything about it. The storm represents a hopeless situation.

In first century Jewish culture, control of nature was attributed exclusively to God. Remember the story of Elijah and his confrontation with the prophets of Baal? Baal worshippers believed that Baal controlled the weather. Elijah's prophetic proclamation that God was sending rain to end the three-year drought got the attention of the people—as the rain fell, they knew Jehovah was God (1 Kings 17–18).

At one time, signs posted alongside the western shore of the Sea of Galilee warned drivers of the dangers of high winds. This large lake can become very rough, producing big waves that can swamp cars parked on what looked like a safe beach. Boats can get "suddenly tossed" around like toy boats—the lake can become ferocious like an ocean in a storm. The disciples were in a "great windstorm," and confidence in what God spoke gave way to fear.

The storm was filling the boat with water—this is fact. Faith doesn't deny facts, but it declares the power of God in the face of problems. The storm was a reality, but there is a greater reality to live from—Christ in you! Circumstances, resistance, and spiritual warfare happen in this life. You must learn to live from His victory—your enthroning with Christ. Jesus gave Himself for you, for His Church that He loves.

Paul declared, *"...Christ loved the church and gave himself for her."* (Eph. 5:25 CEB) You are completely accepted, adopted, forgiven, valued and honored by God. You must receive God's love, love yourself as He loves you, and love others with His love. The Father sees you as you really are, a new creation in Christ.

The blood of Christ removes sin and cleanses you from unrighteousness. The Spirit transforms you. Consider what the writer of Hebrews stated, *"I will never again remember their sins and lawless deeds."* (Heb. 10:17 NLT)

Your ability to rest in the finished work of Christ (rest in what He has accomplished) and remain in the Father's love affects how victorious you live your life. Paul explains how steadfast God's love is, *"Three things will last forever—faith, hope, and love—and the greatest of these is love."* (1 Cor. 13:13 NLT) Love transforms us, faith and hope sustain us. It's been said that "faith is the anchor to our souls." True.

So, what does the enemy attack? Primarily, he attacks our faith, hope, and love. He attempts to rob you of steadfast faith and trust in God, by doubting the goodness of God and the power of His promises. He attempts to rob you of a future filled with hope and joy, and he tries to rob you of true love through counterfeit affections and emotions.

Without fail, when you act on what God has directed you to do, the enemy will bring circumstances to try and stop you. Jesus has defeated all power and authority of the enemy—He is the ruling king now!

Satan only has power over us to the degree that we agree with his lies. When we agree with poverty, sickness, or defeat we live there. But God's gift of faith says, "No, you're an heir of God and joint-heir with Christ. You have a heavenly inheritance available now—believe and make a withdrawal from heaven's account!" When you refuse fear, you cause the enemy to tremble.

Faith is a revelation to the heart of the revealed will of God. God's revealed will creates faith and empowers us to risk. Evening on the water is risky, but faith is willing to risk as God leads. It's often during the storms that His grace is the strongest in our lives.

Faith verses Fear in an Ambulance

"911, what is your emergency?" the dispatcher asked. I responded, "I think I'm having a heart attack." I never thought I would say those words. But my chest was pounding with severe pain, and I knew something was terribly wrong. Wisely, I called for help.

It was 1:30am. The dispatcher asked for my location and said the paramedics would be there in 20 minutes. I was alone and away from home in a hotel room in Dayton, Ohio. I had flown in early to attend a seminary graduation with my students the following day. I called Carolyn prior to calling 911 to tell her what I was experiencing. We both agreed that I should call for help. Until the paramedics arrived, I called Carolyn back and stayed on the phone with her. We prayed and waited for help to arrive—it would be a long night for both of us.

The paramedics asked a couple of questions, placed me on a gurney, and took me outside to the ambulance. They inserted an IV, took an EKG, and gave me medication. My blood pressure was very low, so they gave me something to increase it. When they did, the pain in my chest increased dramatically. The pain was intense before, but now it was almost unbearable.

I prayed quietly, "Jesus, I need your help." No sooner than I whispered those words, I saw Jesus with my mind's eye standing next to me in the ambulance. He said to me, "You have a blockage in your heart, but you are going to be okay." He then smiled and continued, "You are going to live for many more years!" Jesus didn't take the chest pains away, but I had His peace and His assurance everything would be okay, and I had a future to believe for.

You see, God is with us always, and ready to answer our prayers in the most severe of situations, but His answer may not come as we desire. Jesus revealed Himself to me and gave His word that I would be okay and live for many more years—which was wonderful and amazing. But in that moment, what I thought I needed most was the chest pains to go away. For reasons we won't understand on this side of eternity, the pain didn't leave my chest. Instead, I had His peace in a "storm" because I had His presence and His word.

The foundation of our faith is to trust God always, even when we can't see clearly because of the darkness surrounding us. Honestly, if I could have "answered my own prayer," God would have taken away my pain and healed my heart instantly. But He didn't. Does that make Him any less loving, good, or powerful? No! When life's circumstances don't go the way we expect, and our minds remain unrenewed, we will doubt God's goodness and love. True faith leans on God always, not on our human reasoning or understanding of circumstances (Prov. 3:5–6).

After the encounter with Jesus, the atmosphere shifted in the ambulance—confusion left, and clarity prevailed. I leaned over to the paramedic on my left and simply said, "I have a blockage in my heart, please get me to the hospital quickly." He responded, "Yes, I agree," and told the driver to get to Miami Valley Hospital in Dayton ASAP.

I've never been in an ambulance, and by His grace never plan to be in one again, but that ride to the hospital was difficult. The pain radiated from my chest to my upper back, and every bump the ambulance hit in the road caused me to writhe in pain. But I had God's presence and I had His word, despite the pain and what was occurring in the natural.

Once we arrived, I was greeted by several emergency room workers. They rushed me into a room for an emergency heart catheterization procedure. Despite my chest pain and a flurry of activity by the hospital staff, I didn't have any fear, but I did have God's peace. In fact, through the entire evening I never once thought about dying. His presence and peace were tangible. I knew God was at work during my storm.

The heart catheterization procedure went well. The doctor and staff were skilled, proficient, and calm through it all. The pain in my chest and back were still severe, and it was hard to lay on the table, but I trusted God, His ways, and these people I never met before. When the doctor found the primary blockage in my heart, I could literally feel the pressure and pain begin to subside as he placed the stent in place. He found another blockage and repeated the process.

After the second stent, all my chest and back pain were gone. I not only felt God's peace, but joy welled up within me—I was elated and smiling! I shook the doctor's hand and thanked him and the staff for their excellent care. The doctor called Carolyn, informing her of the procedure and my excellent progress. Does Jesus still work miracles? Absolutely!

I slept on and off for the next couple of hours in ICU. I had a large picture window to my left, and as the sun rose, I was captivated by the morning beauty. It was as though heaven was breaking in fresh and new. I was elated to see another day and rejoiced in the faithfulness and promise of God, "You will be ok and live for many more years!"

Carolyn, with the help of others, arraigned to fly to Dayton the morning after my procedure, and I was grateful to see her soon. Suddenly, I began to have mild chest pains again. It was mid-morning and the nurse ordered an EKG. Nothing seemed out of the ordinary. Yet, the chest pains continued to increase.

The doctor came by a couple of hours later, and suggested they perform another heart catheterization procedure to ensure nothing was missed. While the nurses were prepping me, one of my colleagues and two students from the seminary came by to pray for me. Many were praying in our church and around the globe, which I am grateful for, but as the three of them laid hands on me and prayed, something shifted. They hugged me, said their goodbyes, and the nurses took me to the heart cath lab.

The doctor and team performed another cath procedure but did not discover any other blockage or damage to the heart that would be causing the pain. They finished the procedure and I was taken back to my room in ICU. Ironically, as suddenly as the pain began that morning, it was gone, and I've not had any chest pain since. Perhaps the doctor going back into my heart and probing with the cath wire loosened something, but even the doctor was unsure why the pain suddenly started and later disappeared as quickly. However, I am convinced of the power and effectiveness of all who were praying!

Carolyn arrived later that day, followed by my daughter, Hannah, and son-in-law, Tyler. I was recovering well; so well in fact, the doctor said I could be released on Sunday. At the doctor's directive, we stayed in Dayton for three days before flying home to Tucson. We made the most of our time in Dayton, but I knew there was much hard work ahead for a full recovery. Once home, I began my new cardiac diet and cardio exercise regime—no time to waste. Jesus said I would live "many more years," but I knew I had to do my part.

Within a month, I had lost 20lbs and was feeling stronger. The echocardiogram taken one month after the heart attack showed my heart with an EF of 60 (EF or ejection fraction, is a measurement of the percentage of blood leaving your heart, normal is 60–65). When I had the heart attack, the cardiologist doing the cath procedure measured my EF at 40. In one month, my heart EF was showing normal! My family doctor simply said, "It's a miracle!" By the end of the summer, I was jogging four times a week, feeling strong, and lost 40lbs total—by His grace!

Jesus was with me in the ambulance, through the challenging night, and the days of recovery following. You can trust Him, even when you don't understand the "whys?" of the circumstances in life.

Jesus is with You Always—Period!
Keep in mind, Jesus is with you always. This is not a cliché point—it's an accomplished fact. You are completely united with Christ even on your worst day! I can testify to this reality.

A glorious, advancing church takes her directives from heaven. She isn't focused on circumstances or world events; she listens to the master's voice. Our destiny is to progressively enter the glory of God prepared for us before the foundation of the world. You are a vessel of mercy and power—it's your high calling.

Too many people are hindered by their past. Your past is not a prophecy of your future. God has good things for you if you dare to believe His word. The path of the righteous is like the dawn—your path is brighter each day!

Jesus is at Rest
Mark records the "rest of Jesus" during the storm, *"38 But He was in the stern, asleep on a pillow. And they awoke Him and said to Him, "Teacher, do You not care that we are perishing?" 39 Then He arose and*

rebuked the wind, and said to the sea, "Peace, be still!" And the wind ceased and there was a great calm." (Mark 4:38–39)

During chaos, Jesus is at rest, confident in the Father's presence and power. The story contrasts the panic of the disciples, He is at rest—they are in distress. The disciples saw the situation and fear seized them. In their minds, God was distant, and it appeared He didn't care. Have you ever had a moment like this, where a situation caused you to panic and fear the worst? Most of us have at some point in our lives.

But Jesus rose and "rebuked the wind." Rebuked is from Greek word *epitimaō*, and it is also used to describe casting out unclean spirits in Mark 1:25; 3:12, perhaps suggesting demonic powers caused the storm. *Epitimaō* means "to command, with the implication of a threat."[1] Jesus was not just threatening the wind, but the powers of darkness attempting to thwart their mission. For the Jews, the sea came to symbolize the dark power of evil. For example, in Daniel 7 monsters come forth from the sea. Keep in mind Jesus has defeated the enemy and destroys evil (1 John 3:8).

Learning to discern the nature of storms and circumstances is important, it affects how you pray. Some situations are ordained by God—you can't rebuke this kind of storm. Other circumstances are a result of natural events or forces beyond our control, such as wars, natural disasters, equipment failing, etc. Generally, you can't "rebuke" these situations either, but you can learn how to trust God during these challenges, remain in His peace, and pray with confidence. But there is a place for prayer or decree to combat the powers of darkness behind certain storms, like war, pandemics, famine etc. Again, discernment is needed.

Remember the story of Jonah in the Bible? In Jonah 1:5–6, we read how he slept while the pagan sailors fought for survival on board the ship. A first century hearer of Mark's account of Jesus in the storm would have remembered Jonah's story. Jonah could have tried to "rebuke the storm," but God was orchestrating events to bring Jonah into His perfect will—going to Nineveh. However, in Mark's story, Jesus isn't fleeing—He is at rest—confident in the Father's directive and will.

At the end of Mark 5, we read of the resurrection of Jarius' daughter. Jesus states, "The child is not dead but asleep," and proceeds to raise her back to life. Therefore, in the presence of Jesus, things may not be as they appear naturally. You see, with Jesus, hopelessness is an opportunity for a miracle—faith triumphs fear!

Jesus is asleep, secure in the Father. It doesn't mean He is unconcerned about their situation—He is operating in peace. But the disciples awaken Jesus, "Teacher, do you not care that we are perishing?" They assume God doesn't care about their storm. They quickly forgot the times Jesus kept evil from coming against them. We often do the same.

Jesus Equates Fear with little Faith

Mark continues, *⁴⁰ But He said to them, "Why are you so fearful? How is it that you have no faith?" ⁴¹ And they feared exceedingly, and said to one another, "Who can this be, that even the wind and the sea obey Him!"* (Mark 4:40–41)

The disciples fear for two reasons. First, their natural knowledge of the sea and the terror of the moment clouds their faith perspective. Secondly, they fear the raw power of God at work through Jesus, *"Who can this be, that even the wind and sea obey Him!"* They fear the very presence of God.

By asking them, *"Why are you so fearful (or afraid)? Do you still have no faith?"* Jesus reverses their question (teacher, don't you care?), instead putting them on the spot in Mark 8, *"Don't you yet have faith?"*

Fear Due to Natural Knowledge and Circumstances

The disciples feared because they had more confidence in their knowledge of the sea than they had trust in Jesus. Fear results when sensory knowledge overrides the Spirit inspired revelation of Jesus and His promises. In other words, when natural knowledge based on our senses and circumstances outweighs our trust in God, we are reacting from a position of fear rather than faith. When Jesus contrasts fear with faith, He equates fear with underdeveloped faith and lack of confidence in Him.

Fear will try and convince you there is no hope—you are perishing—it's over. Perhaps it's the doctor's report, your bank account, a layoff notice, your marriage, the wayward child, your past, etc. Others fear loss, loneliness, and lack. Some fear the future, and many fear death. But, for the Christian, Jesus is our hope, He is our confidence through every season and circumstance we face—including global pandemics, war, and famine.

As God reveals His will for a situation, fear can prevent you from acting in faith. Do you remember the story of the twelve spies in Numbers 13? Twelve spies, one man from each of the tribes of Israel, were sent by Moses into the promised land to prepare the people to take possession of God's promise.

The twelve return and only Joshua and Caleb were confident to take the land of promise (Num. 13:27–33). They saw how good the land was, *"A land that truly flows with milk and honey."* Caleb declared, *"Let's go now and take procession of the land, we can do this!"* The other ten spies who came out of Canaan said, *"We are not able to go up against the people there…"* Their negative report created fear in a nation that day. Except for Joshua and Caleb forty years later, a fearful generation missed their opportunity.

Fear replaced faith within the ten spies and eventually all of Israel, *"…were like grasshoppers in our own sight, and so we were in their sight."* Fear robbed a nation of their inheritance, and fear can rob you and I of God's gifts and promises. God already gave them the land of Canaan, but fear masqueraded as human reasoning and faith was rejected.

Always remember Paul's admonition to his disciple, Timothy, *"For God has not given us a spirit of fear, but of power and of love and of a sound mind."* (2 Tim. 1:7) Timothy was overseer of the church of Ephesus during severe persecution and trial. He was reminding Timothy, and us today, to refuse fear and trust God during trials. God's love and power keep and preserve us during the darkest night. You have the mind of Christ—remain steadfast and confident in Him!

Fear of God's Presence

The phrase, *"Why are you so fearful?"* is in the present tense and could read, "Why are you afraid now?" In this story and in Mark 5:15 with the deliverance of the demonized man of the Gadarenes, the disciples are afraid of being in the presence of Jesus, who has control over nature, the storms, and demons.

Jesus equated the disciples fear with faithlessness. They lacked confidence in the power of God working through Jesus. Why? Their hearts weren't transformed by His presence and truth He had revealed. Hearts can only be changed in Jesus's presence as you gaze upon His face and abide in His word. God's Word is truth, it is active and alive, but it must actively be received.

Growth involves cultivation of the heart with the seed of God's truth. It is watered by the presence of the Holy Spirit as you allow Him to lead you. The seed has power, but the farmer must cooperate with the life in the seed. You and I must cultivate God's promises in our hearts to see a fruitful harvest of faith.

By the way, the fear of God's presence is nothing new. Do you remember the story of the children of Israel in the wilderness? They were fearful of God's presence at Mount Sinai. They told Moses to speak to them, instead of hearing from God directly, because they feared death in His presence (Exodus 20:18–19). However, the Father wanted a nation of priests, those who would love Him, listen to Him, and serve Him out of obedient delight—not fear.

Through Jesus, we can continually abide in God's presence and hear His voice. We are not to fear God but to abide in His presence confidently (John 15). We need to renew our minds and focus by abiding in God's presence and meditating upon God's Word.

In Psalm 16, David gives us key principles for resting confidently in God during the storms of life. First, he declares, *"Preserve me, O God, for in You I put my trust."* (Psalm 16:1)

1) Security is discovered in confident trust of God.

Then in Psalm 16:8 David's says, *"I have set the Lord always before me; Because He is at my right hand I shall not be moved."* David is declaring (my paraphrase), "I have set the Lord before my face or gaze… therefore I am secure!" By the way, Peter references this verse in his Pentecost sermon resulting in the salvation of 3,000 (Acts 2:14–41).

Jesus promised we would see Him, *"A little while, and you will not see Me; and again a little while, and you will see Me, because I go to the Father."* (John 16:16) Therefore, we should

2) Expect to "see" the Lord!

The way we see (or perceive) the Lord is by following David's example, "I have set the Lord always before me." The Holy Spirit makes us aware of God's presence, His glory, to those who believe and seek Him.

Unfortunately, many misdirect their attention upon themselves, rather than upon pleasing the Lord. The result of which is that they fear God's presence and lack confidence in the storms of life. Finally, we should

3) Set Him before us always.

When we make the pursuit of Jesus and His presence our priority, we won't fear His presence and have more poise during the challenges of life.

Keep in mind that there is a "reverential fear of the Lord," that fosters faith. God is our friend and we have the privilege to draw near to Him confidently through the grace of Christ (Heb. 4:16). But God is also our Father, and we should also come to Him in sincerity of heart and reverential honor (Prov. 1:7; Ps. 111:10, Matt. 6:9, Luke 11:2).

Don't set the Lord aside for access just in emergencies! Rather, set the Lord before your face always—enjoy His presence, His Word, worship, and prayer. Live out of your divine union with Jesus, out of a love relationship with the King of Kings.

The Antidote to Fear is Confident Trust in God

Proverbs addresses the fear syndrome, *"The fear of man brings a snare, but whoever trusts in the Lord shall be secure."* (Prov. 29:25) The English word for *trust* in this verse is translated from the Hebrew *bā·ṭăḥ*, which means to trust, rely on, put confidence in, i.e., believe in a person or object to the point of reliance upon. It also means to make someone a refuge.[2] We could read Prov. 29:25 like this, "Whoever makes the Lord their refuge shall be secure."

David in Psalm 57 writes of this type of trust, where God is a refuge, *"Be merciful to me, O God, be merciful to me! For my soul trusts in You; And in the shadow of Your wings I will make my refuge, until these calamities have passed by."* (Psalm 57:1) David wrote this psalm when he fled from Saul to hide in a wilderness cave. David was in a hard place in his life—wrongly accused, persecuted, and fearing for his life. Yet, he learned how to trust God in a storm.

The psalm imagines David nestling under God's care for refuge, in the same manner that a defenseless and trusting baby bird hides itself under its parent's feathers. We weather the storms of life secure in God has our refuge, our hope, and life. This type of faith and confidence develop through daily abiding in God's presence.

Jesus was at rest in His union with the Father and the Holy Spirit, and He spoke directly to the wind—cease—and to the sea—"be still." Our union with Christ, resting in His finished work affords us the same authority and confidence. God should not be merely an addendum to our lives, but confident faith develops when God is truly our refuge.

Trials, suffering, and storms in life come to all of us. Jesus' authority is without limit, and though God allows trials, in the end, nothing can truly harm those who trust in Him (Luke 10:19).

When you don't sense God's presence, press into Him even more. Set Jesus before your face continually. Praise Him in the tough times like you would in the good times, which is possible when you have learned to set the Lord before your face always. David could confidently state, *"You will show me the path of life; In Your presence is fullness of joy; At Your right hand are pleasures forevermore."* (Psalm 16:11) He learned the secret of abiding in the shelter of the most high.

Jesus is our greatest joy and our peace, His *"perfect love casts out fear."* (1 John 4:18) Your ability to rest in God and His promises will keep you free from fear and worry during the most difficult circumstances and storms in life. Allow Him to be your refuge, because it is the birthplace of faith overcoming fear!

Chapter Two

Help My Unbelief

"Immediately the father of the child cried out and said with tears, "Lord, I believe; help my unbelief!" Mark 9:24

"The greatest weakness in the world is unbelief. The greatest power is the faith that worketh by love." Smith Wigglesworth

Do you remember film cameras? Some of you may even remember box film cameras—I'm dating myself! Today, digital photography has largely replaced film camera photography, except in certain professional applications. You may recall that with film cameras, dark rooms were required to develop the film negatives.

The photography class I took in high school required spending a considerable amount of time in the dark room to develop the film negatives from my 120mm camera. Learning how to develop the negatives in a dark room was challenging, but when they developed correctly, it was immensely rewarding.

Here's a related thought…in darkness, negatives are developed. Using our film camera analogy, unbelief could be likened to a dark room. I've heard it said, *"Unbelief is the dark room where you develop your negatives!"* In difficult circumstances, hopelessness thrives on negativity. Conversely, faith develops in the light of God's presence and Word. Light dispels not only the darkness but the negativity that develops.

Help My Unbelief

In Mark's gospel, there is a story about a man who had a demonized son. He pleads with Jesus, *"Lord I believe, help my unbelief!"* (Mark 9:14–29) But this story occurs after Jesus is transfigured on the mountaintop. Descending the mountain, Jesus, Peter, James, and John discover the other disciples are surrounded by a large crowd. The scribes, who had previously argued with Jesus about exorcisms (Mark 3:22), are now doing the same with disciples.

Looking at Jesus, the crowd is utterly amazed and drawn to Him (Mark 9:15). Like Moses radiating God's glory, (Exod. 34:29), Jesus emanates God's glory. By the way, something tangible occurs as we spend time in God's presence—His presence and glory lingers with us!

Jesus asks, *"What are you arguing about?"* (Mark 9:16) Coming forward to explain, a man from the crowd brings his son, possessed by a mute spirit, to Jesus for help.[1] Not only is the boy speechless but the demon doesn't speak either, unlike other cases in Mark (Mk 1:24, 34; 5:7).

The man justifiably expected Jesus' power to be exercised by the disciples, since they had been delegated His authority over evil spirits (Mark 6:7). Although the disciples had successfully used their delegated authority over demons on previous occasions (Mark 6:13), in this instance they are unsuccessful and confused.

Jesus expresses His frustration with the persistent unbelief of the disciples and people, *"O faithless generation, how long will I be with you?"* (Mark 9:19) After all the signs and miracles they have witnessed, Jesus calls them *faithless*, or literally *unbelieving*. It appears that His frustration was not only with the disciples but also the crowd. Despite all that the disciples had seen—being close to Jesus throughout His teaching and ministry—they are virtually the same as the unbelieving people. It wouldn't be until Pentecost that things truly change, as the disciples are transformed by the power of the Spirit poured out. Communion with the Holy Spirit releases faith and power in our lives!

The disciples bring the boy to Jesus and the spirit within him manifests. The boy falls, rolls around, and foams at the mouth. Even today, this is a common occurrence with those who are severely demonized. The demonized frequently experience physical, and usually painful, manifestations when God's presence is near.

Cautious Faith

The boy's father says to Jesus, *"But if you can do anything, have compassion on us and help us."* (Mark 9:22) Jesus responds, *"If you can believe, all things are possible to him who believes."* (Mark 9:23) The man expressed a cautious faith, hoping for a miracle. But

Jesus turns his tentative question into a challenge to have confident faith. You see, *"If Jesus can..."* is never in question—He is the Great I Am—all things are possible through Him!

In Mark 6, we read an interesting account of the people of Nazareth, *"And because of their unbelief, he couldn't do any miracles among them except to place his hands on a few sick people and heal them. And he was amazed at their unbelief."* (Mark 6:5–6 NLT) Notice that the corporate unbelief of the people of Nazareth limited the miracle working power of Jesus. There is no limit to His authority and power. The only limitation is the barrier of unbelief. Unbelief enables negativity to thrive! And so, the man cries out with tears, *"Lord I believe; help my unbelief!"* (Mark 9:24)

Believe is from the Greek word *pisteúō*, which means to believe to the extent of complete trust and reliance, to have confident trust in a superior authority.[2] The man is attempting to express his confident faith but acknowledges his need for an increase of faith. Throughout the age of the Church, this is a common dilemma. We want to believe, but our human reasoning and anti-miracle bias inhibit us from deep faith in Jesus and belief in the supernatural.

Jesus now demonstrates the greatness of his power and of God's kingdom. The crowd is growing, and Jesus commands the evil spirit out of the young man. The spirit cries out, leaves him, and the boy appears "dead." Jesus takes him by the hand and the boy stands—a miracle! (Mark 9:25–27).

The disciples privately ask Jesus why they couldn't cast the demon out. They have cast out demons before and are confused as to why their method didn't work. Jesus states, *"This kind can come out by nothing but prayer and fasting."* (Mark 9:28–29) Jesus' reply implies that they had lost sight of the need to depend completely on God and not on themselves.

Some ancient manuscripts add "and fasting." Some believe this addition is due to an early Christian view rooted in Jewish piety that prayer is inseparable from self-denial through fasting (Luke 2:37; Acts 13:2–3). David echoes this practice, *"...I humbled myself with fasting."* (Psalm 35:13) A lifestyle of prayer and fasting keep our hearts humble and yielded to God. Fasting doesn't "twist God's arm" into answering prayer. Rather, fasting keeps us close to the heart of God while in prayer. We are more sensitive to hear from the Lord while in communion with Him.

In life and ministry, all fruitfulness flows from our relationship and communion with God. We have the authority of His name and His Word, but the Holy Spirit is the one who releases the power of heaven in and through us as we remain in Him.

Faith is Superior to Unbelief

Everyone loves mountaintop experiences with God, but our encounters with God should lead us to the valley to minister to the hurting. God calls us to reach the lost and the broken-hearted with His love and power. As Jesus transfigured before them, Peter wanted to remain on the mountain, but Jesus knew they needed to return to the valley to minister to the people. Remember the "go therefore" in the Great Commission? (Matt. 28:18–20).

We are His ambassadors and ministers of reconciliation, letting the world know that God in Christ is reconciling the world to Himself (2 Cor. 5). Unbelief has always plagued humanity, including Jesus' own disciples, but the man's humble confession, *"Help my unbelief!"* allows the grace of God to flow. Faith develops through humility.

I believe many are trying to have faith in faith itself. Asking God for help is not a denial of faith. He is a loving Father, not a harsh judge or unkind friend. Approach Jesus humbly and honestly, "Lord, I need help, remove the unbelief and fill me with your faith!" The writer of Hebrews speaks of this, *"Let us therefore come boldly to the throne of grace, that we may obtain mercy and find grace to help in time of need."* (Heb. 4:16)

Jesus said, *"If you can believe, all things are possible to him who believes."* (Mark 9:23) Notice the *all* in *all?* Truly, *all* things are possible with God.

For Jesus, impossibilities are the atmosphere for faith to thrive. Insurmountable obstacles did not intimidate Jesus, and He did not want His disciples intimidated either. Jesus desires His followers to look at situations with God's perspective. Faith and expectation can change even the most daunting of circumstances.

Healing in a Jacuzzi

While on vacation with my family a few years ago, I was using the hot tub at the resort. An older gentleman, who had limited mobility in his right leg, also got in for a therapeutic soak. I began to visit with him and eventually asked him about his leg. He explained to me that he was a retired policeman and had injured his right knee on the job, and he needed surgery to replace it. He shared that this hot tub treatment was a last-ditch effort to alleviate his pain and salvage his golf round the next morning.

I explained to him that I was a follower of Jesus, and that He still heals today through ordinary believers. I asked if I could pray for his knee, and he gave me a skeptical look, but he was desperate enough to play golf that he let me pray for him—in the resort jacuzzi! I prayed a short commanding prayer and asked him to try and move his knee to see if he had greater mobility and less pain.

His face looked shocked, and he said to me, "All the pain is gone, and I can move it again normally!" I said, "Great! Jesus just healed you; He loves you and cares about you." To that the man said, "Yes, I know Jesus does, and I plan on telling others what He did for me!" I encouraged him to go play golf the next day, trusting that God had healed his knee. Two days later, he found me in the restaurant and told me how well his knee was doing and how well his round of golf went. He was healed and grateful for what Jesus did. You see, faith works through love, and God gets the glory.

Ministry is realized through relationship with Jesus resulting in confident faith. Any ministry seeking to bring healing, freedom and wholeness is not a set of steps or formula. We must learn to hear God and follow the Lord's leading as we minister. Prayer, which is communion with God, enables divine dialogue and strengthens faith.

Prov. 25:11 states, *"A word fitly spoken is like apples of gold in settings of silver."* To hear and see the subtle impressions, words, and visions that God reveals are as precious as gold set in the rich silver of our redemption. God speaks in order to strengthen us and build confidence to believe for His miracle power.

Do Not Be Afraid, Only Believe

One of the most perplexing things we can face is when a loved one is ill, and the doctors are unsure what is causing the condition. Despite our modern age of medicine and technology, there are some conditions that are difficult to diagnose and disease that can be incurable. However, Jesus specializes in difficult situations—only believe! Over the years I've witnessed first-hand, or heard reliable testimonies of others, of those who have received miracle healings. It doesn't stop with healing either. I've heard or witnessed many testimonies of marriages healed, families restored, and financial breakthrough to name a few others.

In Mark 5, there are two interrelated stories that demonstrate God's miraculous power and of the necessity for us to replace our fear with belief: the dying twelve-year-old daughter of Jairus and of the woman with the bleeding disorder for twelve years. Their stories illustrate how God can intervene in the direst of circumstances.

As we examined in chapter one, Jesus calms the stormy sea of Galilee and the terrified disciples exclaim, *"Who can this be, that even the wind and the sea obey Him!"* (Mark 4:41) Mark answers this question with three miracle stories in Mark 5 and leaves no room for the reader to misunderstand. The liberation of the demonized man, the healing of the woman with the issue of blood and raising the daughter of Jarius from the dead all convey one simple and profound truth—Jesus is Lord over all! His words to Jairus encourage each of us during the trials of life, *"Do not be afraid, only believe."* (Mark 5:36)

After the healing of the demonized man in the region of Gadara, Jesus crosses to the western shore of Galilee, and Mark records two more miracle stories (Mark 5:21–43). These accounts are linked and further help to answer the question of Mark 4:41, *"Who can this be?"*

The woman has the bleeding condition for twelve years and is near death shares the timeline and dire circumstance of the little girl who is twelve and dying. Unlike the woman, the little girl dies but is soon raised back to life as Jesus takes her hand. The woman, on the other hand, reaches her hand to Jesus. Desperation also links these two stories. Jairus is desperate for his daughter to be healed, and the woman with the bleeding condition pushes through the crowd, risking further ostracization from her Jewish community, in order to receive healing.

Additionally, the theme of "uncleanness" connects these stories. Jesus touches the dead child and is touched by the woman with a bleeding disorder. However, His touch made the "unclean" clean. In Mark 7, we will discover what truly makes one clean or unclean—issues of the heart—not one's outward condition or lack of religious ritual.

Jesus is Societies Equalizer

Like the demonized man of the Gadarenes, Jairus falls at the feet of Jesus publicly. He was a man of wealth and position in the community. The woman with the bleeding disorder also falls at the feet of Jesus a few minutes later. Although the Jairus and the woman are set apart by differing social situations, they are united in their personal need of God's presence and miracle power.

I was reminded of the Azusa Street Revival of 1906 in Los Angeles, CA. The outpouring led to many who were saved, baptized by the Holy Spirit, and who were healed—some receiving creative miracles. The revival was also noted for its diversity.

The rich, poor, black, white, Hispanic, Asian, uneducated, and educated—all sought Jesus in this humble setting on Azusa

Street. God's presence was tangible, and immense joy flowed from the hearts of those who attended. Yet, amidst this mighty outpouring of God's Spirit, newspapers and other critics of the revival mocked it. One of the criticisms was the "intermingling of the races." How sad! Jesus breaks down every wall and barrier. People who are desperate for God and in need of a miracle typically don't erect walls that divide—they come in humility.

Consider Jairus begging Jesus to come heal his daughter—he is desperate. Jesus responds to his plea and goes to his home. Perhaps there is no greater sorrow for a parent than a dying child. Jairus was willing to risk his position and reputation to petition Jesus. Desperation causes even the most affluent to cry out to God for help.

How desperate are we for the children of our cities? Some of them are near death, literally and figuratively. What if we cried out in intercession for those suffering in our communities? Do we hear the cry of those desperate for a miracle?

The Unclean are Made Clean by Jesus

As the crowd follows Jesus and presses in upon Him, the unclean woman approaches Jesus and receives her miracle. Her bleeding condition of twelve years (perhaps from fibroid tumors) caused her to be isolated from Jewish society. Lev. 15:19–33 addresses this type of impurity: people were to avoid any kind of contact with a woman with this disorder. Mark portrays her as being a complete outcast in every respect. She is unable to approach people and ceremonially unfit to approach God. According to Lev. 20, if she were married, there could be no sexual contact with her husband. Scripture says she spent everything she had seeking treatment, to no avail.

Think of it, in addition to her lengthy physical ordeal, she has the shame and stigma of being an outcast and is rejected by her family and society. But then she hears that Jesus is near. She braves the crowd and comes from behind to touch His cloak, thinking, *"If I only may touch His clothes, I shall be made well."* (Mark 5:28) We don't know when she first heard about this miracle worker, but when she learns of Jesus, hope and faith motivate her to action. What if the Church shared the good news of Jesus with the same boldness? What if the church testified of the great works He still does today? Hope would return to many in society—many who need a miracle.

It was believed at the time that "great personalities," such as Elijah, had the power to heal, and since their clothing was an extension of themselves, it too held power. For example, we read in Acts 19:11-12 how many were healed and delivered of demons just from clothing articles from the Apostle Paul. There is a "tangible" presence of God's Spirit and the anointing (smearing) that the Holy Spirit placed on Jesus and upon those who follow Him.

Notice in this story, that immediately upon touching Jesus, "she knew in her body that she had been healed." Jesus also knew that power "had gone out" from Him, which in the Greek is in past participle form and means "no longer happening." Jesus then asks, *"Who touched My clothes?"* (Mark 5:30)

For the second time in these miracle accounts, the disciples are abrupt with Jesus (Mark 4:38; 5:31). *"Look Jesus, you're in a huge crowd and you are wondering who touched you!"* They miss the point of His question, for He is really asking, *"Who touched me in faith?"* But they are responding with human reasoning and understanding. Jesus, however, recognized that a person of faith had encountered Him—faith is the connector to God and His power.

Jesus doesn't instantly recognize the person of faith who touched His clothes. Imagine His piercing eyes, gazing through the crowd as He asks, *"Who touched me?"* In fear, the healed woman falls at his feet—hoping for mercy. She defiled Jesus by touching Him and is expecting punishment. Religion makes the unclean fear judgment, but in Jesus, all fear of judgment is removed.

Instead, He said to her, *"Daughter, your faith has made you well (sozo). Go in peace (shalom), and be healed of your affliction."* (Mark 5:34) She is healed holistically and can participate fully in the covenant life of God's people. Faith not only heals her but restores her to community.

The Tumors are Gone!

I once prayed for a woman who had five large, painful fibroid tumors. She was scheduled for surgery a few weeks later and desperate for the pain to cease and the tumors to disappear. There was a word of knowledge given in the meeting that night about fibroid tumors, and she jumped to her feet believing for her healing.

I saw her stand and approached her and her husband to pray for healing. After praying with her for a few minutes, tears began to stream down her face. She began to exclaim, "All the pain is gone, and I can't feel the tumors any longer!" I encouraged her to go to her doctor to verify, but this woman "felt" in her body God's healing touch. The lumps and pain were gone. She was desperate for her healing and had faith Jesus would heal her. She wasn't disappointed! Her desperation for God's healing touch elevated her faith to receive her healing.

Why Trouble the Teacher

While Jesus is still speaking to the woman, people arrive and give Jairus the sad news, *"Your daughter is dead. Why trouble the teacher?"* (Mark 5:35) Jesus ignores their report and says to Jairus, *"Do not be afraid; only believe."* (Mark 5:36) Here is the great news: Jesus wants to be *troubled!* Truthfully, we don't *trouble* Him often enough! Cry out to Him, expect Him to heal, deliver, and save—it's never hopeless with God.

This passage literally reads, *"Jesus refused to listen to the words they were saying."* Throughout Mark, discernment is a key to understanding. We measure what we hear ... are we measuring fear or faith? One of the secrets to discovering the movement of God in our midst is with the ability to listen and discern which voices are contrary to the truth of the Kingdom of God. Fear often masquerades as truth and reason.

Jesus immediately challenges the human "reasoning" that is creating hopelessness. Ultimately, faith and hope are connected, and Jesus doesn't allow room for fear. Without giving the father time to grieve, Jesus states, *"Do not be afraid, only believe!"* (Mark 5:36) Contrary to human reasoning, Jesus states not to fear death.

Don't Let Emotions Steer Your Faith

When they arrive at Jairus house, "professional" mourners are wailing loudly. No doubt, seeing the turmoil at his home, Jairus faith must have been greatly tested. Emotion was vying to set the agenda—not faith. By the way, keep your emotions in check. They often are contrary to what God is doing.

Jesus shifts the attention away from their mourning and declares, *"The child is not dead but sleeping."* (Mark 5:39) Jesus uses a well-known biblical metaphor for death as a catalyst to build the father's faith, but they ridiculed Him. The "they" is most likely these mourners. Tradition required mourners to express great signs and sounds of sorrow. Yet, they are unaware that the Jesus whom they are mocking had silenced a powerful storm, delivered a demonized man, and cured the woman's untreatable illness.

These mourners function out of human reasoning, which is often contrary to God's will (Mark 8:33). Their skepticism and unbelief cause Jesus to remove them from the house. They are faith distractions for the parents and the three disciples.

My First Time Praying for Cancer Healing
The first time I ever prayed for someone with cancer I was in my early 30's. A middle-aged neighbor, Steve, was battling colon cancer. He was stage four, and the doctors gave him and his family little hope of recovery. He was in the hospital being fed through a tube and fading quickly, but the Lord impressed upon me to go and pray for him. I had little training in healing ministry, yet I was confident that if God told me to go and pray for Steve, something would happen.

When I arrived at his room, I could hear the "mourners." There wasn't anyone in the room, but the voice of doubt dominated the atmosphere, seeking to quench my faith. I began to pray with Steve. I asked him if I could lay hands on his abdomen and pray. He agreed and I prayed in faith and Jesus name, commanding the cancerous cells to die, and trusting Jesus for His healing power to be released. Steve thanked me. We talked a little, and I left after a few minutes.

Three days later, Steve was released from the hospital. The doctors were confused. He could eat and was showing signs of improvement! I found out about his release a week later and went to visit Steve at his home. I was ecstatic and confident God was healing Steve. When I arrived, his wife answered the door, and she looked angry.

I asked if I could see Steve, but she declined me a visit with him and began to berate me for giving him unrealistic optimism. She accused me of giving him false hope when he was "clearly" terminally ill and would die. I was shocked and speechless. I politely said goodbye and left. She was full of anger, doubt and unbelief. Within weeks, Steve passed away.

Negativity and skepticism inhibit God's power from working miracles. I believe God miraculously touched Steve, but after going home, he lost his healing due to his home being filled with doubt and negativity from his spouse. Proverbs tells us, *"Death and life are in the power of the tongue..."* (Prov. 18:21). Your words have power! Release words of faith—not doubt and negativity. The latter will inhibit miracles from occurring.

I Say to You Arise!

Jesus takes the little girl by the hand, *"Little girl, I say to you, arise."* (Mark 5:41) Jairus' daughter comes back to life, and Jesus instructs them to give her something to eat! Remember the question the disciples asked in Mark 4, *"Who is this, even the wind and the waves obey him?"* (Mark 4:41) Jesus's words have power over storms, demonic powers, disease, and death!

Jesus's words carry the weight of eternal life and ignoring Him is a rejection of salvation and power. He is the resurrection and the life—nothing is hopeless with God. Only Jesus can heal the incurable and raise the dead to life. Jesus ignores purity rituals and touches the unclean. God isn't affected by human impurity, sin, and disease. Through Jesus and the New Covenant, believers are invited to approach the "unclean," to bring healing and wholeness in the authority of His name (Matt. 10:7–8).

Jesus is no respecter of persons, as these two stories demonstrate (Jairus, a well to do leader and a poor woman afflicted by a horrible disease). Jesus will touch and heal regardless of one's position in life. Mark illustrates that being male, pure, and wealthy is no advantage over being female, unclean, and destitute. In God's kingdom, faith enables everyone to meet Jesus with equality. Hear Jesus' words today, *"Do not be afraid, only believe!"* What is your need?

Chapter Three

Expectant Faith

"The people were filled with expectation..." Luke 3:15 CEB

"Expectancy opens your life to God and puts you in a position to receive salvation, joy, health, financial supply, or peace of mind—everything good your heart longs for, and more!"

ORAL ROBERTS

Faith is tangible. Have you ever ordered something online? When an order is placed online, the buyer is seeing only an image of the real item. There is substance to that image, it represents a product to be purchased and delivered. You, the buyer, have faith that the item you are purchasing will arrive according to the description and image you viewed. You have faith in an image of that which is material and tangible. You "see it" with the eye of faith before it arrives! Faith sees the promise as reality.

Faith maintains hope of the promise made, and God's promises are sure. Faith accepts as reality the manifestation of those promises. While waiting for the promises to become actuality, hope undergirds faith and postures the believer in joyful anticipation. Faith sees what is invisible as reality on earth.

Did Jesus Leave?

After feeding the multitude in Mark 6, Jesus sends the disciples across the Sea of Galilee and departs to the mountain to pray. It's late at night, and the disciples are rowing against the waves. In the absence of Jesus, it probably felt as though God's presence had left them (Mark 6:45–52).

Have you ever felt like these disciples? Where is God in your midnight hour? Following Jesus requires faith that is greater than human reasoning. To be his disciple, you must embrace uncertainty while maintaining hope amidst contradiction.

God is always with you despite what your emotions or feelings indicate. Jesus promised, *"...I am with you always, even to the end of the age."* (Matt. 28:20) God's omnipresence and tangible presence are two distinct characteristics. God's omnipresence is a fact. He is always with us. However, God's tangible or manifest presence is an awareness of Him. We are to live by faith, resting upon God's Word, not just relying upon sensing the presence of the Holy Spirit. It's important to pursue God's presence and value that relationship. Whether you "feel God" or not, you can rest on what He promises in His Word.

Jesus appears walking on the water to the disciples—and they believe He is a ghost. He gets into the boat, the seas calm, and they are amazed beyond measure. Mark writes, *"...they had not understood about the loaves, because their heart was hardened."* (Mark 6:52)

The twelve disciples had traveled with Jesus and seen many miracles. They witnessed a storm calmed, the demonized freed, the sick cured, the dead raised, and had just witnessed the miracle 5,000 men fed.[1] If that wasn't enough, the disciples themselves had been used by God to heal the sick and cast out demons (Mark 6:12-13).

Unfortunately, the disciples were unable to recognize Jesus' full identity because of their dullness of heart and unbelief. The result: they could not apply His power and grace to help them on that stormy Galilean Sea.

Is it possible, these disciples knew Jesus, but really didn't *know* Jesus? That is, they didn't know Jesus as the Christ, the Son of God in human flesh. Today, many claim to be Christian, but I wonder how well they really know Him? Many who claim to know Jesus live in fear and worry instead of confidently trusting in God's care. Is He the great "I Am" or the great "I Was" to you?

Unbelief to Expectant Faith and Miracles

Mark begins chapter six by referencing the unbelief in Nazareth, Jesus' childhood hometown. The Scripture says He could do no miracles due to their unbelief, only healing a few sick (Mark 6:5-6). The implication by Mark is that faith is required to receive from Jesus. We need an "expectant faith," a faith that is anchored in the love and hope of God. The conclusion of chapter 6 says,

⁵³ When they had crossed over, they came to the land of Gennesaret and anchored there. ⁵⁴ And when they came out of the boat, immediately the people recognized Him, ⁵⁵ ran through that whole surrounding region, and began to carry about on beds those who were sick to wherever they heard He was. ⁵⁶ Wherever He entered, into villages, cities, or the country, they laid the sick in the marketplaces, and begged Him that they might just touch the hem of His garment. And as many as touched Him were made well. (Mark 6:53–56)

Jesus and the disciples cross the sea from east to west, arriving in Gennesaret, a fertile plain south of Capernaum. They have only a brief interlude between encounters. Notice, *"… the people recognized Him, and ran through … region."* The English word *recognize* is from the Greek word *epiginōskō*, meaning—to discern something clearly and distinctly, know well, to perceive, to understand.[2] Those who were the closest to Jesus—His family and disciples—did not discern Him properly. Yet, many from the crowd clearly recognized Him.

The people heard the testimonies about Jesus and believed them as true reports. They had an "expectant faith," came to Jesus, and miracles happened. Their expectant faith led them to carry on beds those who were sick to Jesus, much like the four men of faith in Mark 2 who brought their paralyzed friend for healing. Like the story of the woman with the bleeding condition in Mark 5, people begged to touch the hem (or tassels) of His cloak for healing.

This passage in Mark gives us permission to be intentional and persistent when approaching God. Draw near to God, He will draw near to you—pursue Him expectantly.

In Expectation

Luke records, *"Now as the people were in expectation"*—from the Greek *prosdokáō* meaning to wait or look for, to expect—*"and all reasoned in their hearts about John, whether he was the Christ or not."* (Luke 3:15)

Israel had not seen a prophet for 400 years. It was widely believed that when the Messiah would come prophecy would reappear (Joel 2:28–29; Mal. 3:1; 4:5). When John the Baptist burst onto the scene, people were excited and expectant. He was a great prophet, and they were sure the Messianic age had come.

What about you today? Do you have expectant faith? Jesus, the Messiah, the Son of God has come. He has made the way for salvation, healing, and miracles. But faith, as Mark's gospel confirms, is required to receive anything from Jesus.

Twentieth century healing evangelist Oral Roberts said this about expectancy as related to faith, "Expectancy opens your life to God and puts you in a position to receive salvation, joy, health, financial supply, or peace of mind—everything good your heart longs for, and more!" Live expectantly! You will be positioned to receive what God has promised.

Principles for Expectant Faith

The Power of Testimony

The crowds around the region of Galilee heard the stories and testimonies about Jesus. Every healing and miracle story confirmed that Jesus was the Messiah. The result? People's faith increased as they heard the good news! *"So faith comes from hearing, that is, hearing the Good News about Christ."* (Rom. 10:17 NLT)

Rev. 19:10b states, *"...For the testimony of Jesus is the spirit of prophecy."* Every testimony about Jesus and God's power at work releases a glimpse of heaven that creates faith in the hearer. Expectant faith rises, providing a pathway for God to work miraculously again.

The Power of the Word

God's word and Jewish tradition foretold the coming of the Messiah. The people expected miracles to occur when the Messiah came. God's Word and the testimonies of the people created expectant faith in their hearts. The people of Israel started to believe the Messianic Age had arrived. *"Faith is the substance of things hoped for, the evidence of things not seen."* (Heb. 11:1)

Faith is substantive in nature. It sees the promise fulfilled while positioned in hope. Faith expectantly anticipates the promise fulfilled. At its base level, faith is simply trusting God and His Promises. *"But without faith it is impossible to please Him, for he who comes to God must believe that He is, and that He is a rewarder of those who diligently seek Him."* (Heb. 11:6) God honors faith; it pleases Him. Faith moves God's heart. Grace, or empowerment, is released to help us in times of need as we approach God confidently (Heb. 4:16).

The parable of the Sower in Mark 4 explains how God's word is sown. Some seed falls on hard soil and some falls on good ground. We need to understand that there is power in the seed—power in God's promise. But the promises must be heard, believed, and acted upon. *"Then He said to them, "Take heed what you hear. With the same measure you use, it will be measured to you; and to you who hear, more will be given."* (Mark 4:24) More understanding, revelation, and faith will be given to those who hear expectantly and have faith in God's promise.

Faith is the connector to the promises and blessings of God's kingdom. It makes a demand on the promises of heaven, confident that God will release the answer. It is possible to believe a promise, while lacking faith and courage to appropriate it. Smith Wigglesworth, twentieth century healing evangelist known for his strong faith in God's promises, said, "God rejoices when we manifest a faith that holds Him to His Word."

The Need for Action

The people acted on the news of Jesus being in their area. They ran to be in the meetings with Him. They said amongst themselves, "If we can just get our sick loved ones to Jesus, He will heal them!" There was no doubt, just expectant faith followed by action. Faith is demonstrated through obedient action. James 2:18 says, *"I will show you my faith by my works."*

They didn't care how foolish they looked. They ran through the region bringing those who needed a miracle. They positioned themselves to receive from Jesus. In turn, Jesus commends those who approach Him, *"Blessed are the poor in spirit, for theirs is the kingdom of heaven."* (Matt. 5:3) Expectant faith looks odd to those who only believe through their natural knowledge of circumstances.

The Necessity of Intimacy

The people "knew" Jesus and discerned He was the Messiah. Genuine intimacy with Jesus, builds trust to follow Him, faith to obey His commands, and courage to believe His promises. To be filled with the Spirit is to be filled with faith. To prevail in spiritual power requires a lifetime of intimacy and communion with God.

Learn to live out of your divine union with Jesus. *"And because of his glory and excellence, he has given us great and precious promises. These are the promises that enable you to share his divine nature and escape the world's corruption caused by human desires."* (2 Pet. 1:4 NLT)

Live from the reality of the finished work of Christ, resting in His ascension victory and glory. Live from your union with Him and trust His promises. Your life in the Spirit empowers you to see beyond this earthly realm. The sufferings in this life are real but hold onto hope with an expectant faith. Jesus is the resurrection and the life—trust Him! Resurrection life awaits the follower of Christ (1 Cor. 15:20)!

Mountain Moving Faith

A Withered Fig Tree

Jesus enters Jerusalem the week before his crucifixion, and through a fig tree, illustrates important principles about prayer and faith (Mark 11:12-14, 20-26). Keep in mind that faith is the connector to God's Kingdom. It is the key that unlocks heavens resources. It's been said that "faith is the currency of heaven." As you read the story, ponder these questions, "Is faith something we work-up with our human effort?" "Do we obtain more faith by believing harder?"

The following day after his triumphal entry into Jerusalem, Jesus sees a fig tree in the distance and walks toward it. As He gets close, He sees leaves on the tree but no figs. It is not the season for figs, but Jesus nonetheless expects fruit on the tree.

In response to the lack of fruitlessness, Jesus curses the tree, *"Let no one eat fruit from you ever again."* (Mark 11:14)

The next day, He and the disciples pass by the tree again, to find that the fig tree has withered and dried up. Peter remembered and said to Jesus, *"Rabbi, look! The fig tree which You cursed has withered away."* (Mark 11:21) Ultimately, the withered fig tree represents Israel and her unfruitfulness in trying to keep the law. While the law was unfruitful, a new covenant would produce fruit. Jesus is the vine; we are the branches of His life and of His new covenant. Therefore, abiding in the life of Christ assures fruitfulness in every season. Being in season with God demonstrates your maturity and capacity for greater responsibility.

Jesus responds to Peter by saying, *"Have faith in God!"* (Mark 11:22) He explains the power of faith and prayer, *"I assure you that whoever says to this mountain, 'Be lifted up and thrown into the sea'—and doesn't waver but believes that what is said will really happen—it will happen. Therefore I say to you, whatever you pray and ask for, believe that you will receive it, and it will be so for you."* (Mark 11:23-24 CEB)

Faith to move mountains begins with believing God hears your prayers. God is ever present, all knowing, and hears your prayer—always. But what mountain was Jesus referring too? A mountain, as illustrated with the fig tree, is any difficulty, hindrance, or impossible problem you are facing. Jesus demonstrates that faith provides an entry point for God to move amid challenging situations.

But is it true that *"...whatever you pray and ask for believe that you will receive it, and it will be so for you?"* These are the words of Jesus, the perfecter of our faith. Is it possible that some of our prayers are unanswered due to our unbelief? Have we limited God by doubting His promises?

Debt-Free!
Have you ever been concerned about your finances? Most of us have at some point in our lives. Carolyn and I, like many married couples, were concerned about the debt we had incurred. During the fall of 1991, we attended a financial seminar at our church. Prior to the seminar, we read and heard many present-day testimonies of God's miraculous provision. We were confident God would do it again for us. During the seminar, God gave me a word regarding our finances.

The meeting facilitator advised participants to set financial goals, as the starting point to live debt free. That's when God spoke to me. It was not an audible voice, but the Holy Spirit spoke to me, "You will be debt free by October 1st, 1992." I wrote this word on a piece of notebook paper and placed it in my Bible and began to pray over it.

We put into practice some of the biblical financial tools we learned from the seminar and we continued to pray and stand in faith, based on the word we received. We would be debt free by October 1st, 1992.

During the summer of 1992, the Lord instructed us to sell a small franchise business we had started two years prior. By the end of that summer, someone offered to buy the business for twice our original investment. God was moving our "debt mountain" in the unseen realm! Soon, our natural realm would manifest God's plan for this season of our lives.

On October 1st, 1992, we closed on the sale of the business and received a sizable check that paid off all our existing debts!

The remaining funds God used as "seed" money to propel us into ministry and the mission field. It began by understanding God's promises for financial provision in His Word. As we heard the testimonies of others receiving financial breakthrough, our faith increased. Finally, when I received the word from Jesus that we would be debt free, faith was released in our hearts to see our mountain move. We could stand on His promises, other's testimonies, and His personal word to us!

Obtaining Faith from God

Jesus told the man with the tormented son in Mark 9:23, *"If you can believe, all things are possible to him who believes."* Jesus is not speaking of intellectual belief or agreement but a heart-belief that is real faith. Only Jesus can give this type of faith. It is faith involving the heart, not the mind.

Belief is an assurance of the mind; faith is an assurance of the heart. When Jesus said to Peter, *"Come, walk on the water,"* it empowered Peter to act in faith (Matt. 14:28–31). Jesus' directive imparted grace to Peter to look past the natural circumstances and briefly walk on water. Your natural knowledge of situations will move you from faith to doubt every time. Be careful to not lean on what your senses reveal. Many people confuse their mental belief with imparted faith from Jesus.

When our church was two years old, Carolyn and I felt God put on our hearts a desire to find a permanent building for our church. We looked at several storefronts and pieces of property. While some of them looked promising, we didn't have God's peace or a word from Jesus for any of those buildings. You could say that we hadn't heard yet, *"Come, walk on the water!"*

When God's gift of faith is released in your heart, an assurance of answered prayer is discovered. Your prayers for the situation take on new boldness and confidence with God's gift of faith. I love what German evangelist Reinhard Bonnke said, "I don't want to play with marbles when God told me to move mountains!" How true. We are invited to move mountains with Jesus! Why settle for less?

Dr. Charles S. Price, a twentieth century healing evangelist, wrote a terrific book on faith and healing titled, *The Real Faith for Healing* (you can find the pdf on the internet for free). He was touched powerfully by the Holy Spirit in the early part of the twentieth century and became a well-known healing minister. He said in his book, "You can believe a promise, but at the same time not have the faith to appropriate it."[3] This is very true. Many people have mental agreement with God's promises but aren't assured in their hearts of the answer.

Always remember, *"Jesus is the author and finisher of your faith."* (Heb. 12:2) The writer of Hebrews, in mentioning OT heroes of faith in Hebrews 11, is giving us something more than a pattern to follow; we are given a new starting point in Jesus and the New Covenant. The OT cloud of witnesses point to the new race in Christ we are to run. We are to look to Jesus, who originates and completes our faith. All true faith begins and ends with Jesus—the Alpha and Omega.

Jesus is your source of life, your greatest joy, and the motivation to ask audacious requests of the Father. Real faith is rooted in the nature and character of God. As you learn to trust Him more, His faith will be imparted to you. True faith is an expectant anticipation of the reality of the promise before the manifestation. Faith acts upon God's revealed truth with an assurance of the answer.

When I want more faith, I must seek Jesus. Remember the man's cry in Mark, *"Lord I believe, help my unbelief!"* (Mark 9:24) In other words, "Jesus, I need more faith!" You can have God's gift of faith as you learn to keep your focus upon Christ. The moment you take your eyes off of Jesus, you lose sight of the primary goal of your faith. He is the goal, destination, and reason you do what you do. Faith to move mountains begins and ends with Jesus.

Buy This Property!
Remember the church building we were looking for? After looking at multiple properties, God led us to an older Wesleyan Church in central Tucson. I scheduled an appointment with the realtor to view it on a Friday. After walking through the property, I immediately had a peace about it and sensed the Holy Spirit wanted me to make an offer. Carolyn's head was spinning as I shared with her and the realtor that we would make an offer! Looking back on it, I should have cooled my excitement and talked to her first before blurting this out to the realtor.

The next morning, I asked the Lord for a clear word. I needed a word like Peter received about walking on the water, "Come!" I heard the Lord say to me, "This is the property I spoke to you about. Don't look at the size of the sanctuary or how much money is in the church bank account. This property is a building block and steppingstone to the worship and revival center that I have spoken to you about." After receiving this word, God me a gift of faith to purchase the building, with Carolyn soon to follow. We began a faith adventure of believing God for over $500,000 when we only had $2,000 in the church bank account!

Within three months, we raised several thousand dollars, took a second mortgage on our home to help with the down payment, and received a bank loan to purchase the property. In the Spirit, we saw the title deed for the property before we had the property in our possession. Jesus said, "Come!" and gave us His faith for the building. A few months later, we closed on the property. God's word came to pass! I tell the entire story in my previous book, *Fulfill Your Dreams*.

You can have God's gift of faith as you learn to keep your focus upon Jesus. If you want faith to move mountains, learn how to hear, believe, and act upon what Jesus reveals. Real faith comes from Him.

Real faith is rooted in the nature and character of God. As you learn to trust Jesus more, His faith will be imparted to you. I heard Dr. Rolland Baker, a missionary to Africa, say, "Faith is to know Jesus well enough to know what He wants to do in any situation." The same Holy Spirit, who raised Jesus from the dead, lives and abides in you as a follower of Christ. This truth is why Paul could declare with confidence, *"Now to Him who is able to do exceedingly abundantly above all that we ask or think, according to the power that works in us."* (Eph. 3:20)

Chapter Four

Faith from God

> *"So Jesus answered and said to them, "Have faith in God." Mark 11:22*

> *"In New Testament faith, the act can be born of faith, but faith cannot be born of the act. The act can come from faith, but the faith must come from God." Charles S. Price*

There is Faith, and Then There is Faith from God

Often our experience with God and His Word enable us to routinely operate in kingdom authority and power. In other words, we operate at a level of faith developed over time, which is good and effective in many situations. But faith to move mountains requires faith that is beyond our experience and level of understanding of God's Word—we need a gift of faith from God.

A few years ago, I prayed for a desperate woman. That evening, many people were healed of various conditions as the team and I prayed for them. After hours of standing on my feet, I began to tire, and my legs ached. I had one more person to pray for and I would be done. She was a young woman, in her late twenties, with a limp. She had waited in line for hours to receive prayer. She was desperate—she needed a miracle.

After asking her what had happened, she detailed an auto accident a year before, which severely damaged her right knee. Even with reconstructive surgery, she was in constant pain and had little mobility in her knee. I found a chair for her to sit and began to pray. After several minutes of prayer, her condition had not changed. With intense, piercing eyes and a look of desperation unlike any I had seen, she said to me, "Please, if you can do anything, help me!" My heart melted with compassion for her, and I thought to myself, "I can't do anything, but God can. Lord, she needs a miracle, and I need your faith!"

Her faith and desperation tugged on heaven. When we began praying, I was tired and had little faith for her healing, but now a gift of faith was released. The compassion of heaven welled up inside of me as I prayed once more. It was a short commanding prayer in the name of Jesus. I simply commanded all the pain in the knee to leave and for the knee to be restored to new. A surge of God's power was released, which I seldom experience physically as I pray for others.

Just then, she jumped out of the chair and moved her leg without restriction. She shouted, "I'm healed! I'm healed!" All her pain was gone, and she had full range of motion in her knee once again. Her desperation moved Jesus to compassion and his healing power was released.

Faith is the Connector to God's Kingdom

God offers many promises of His presence, protection, and provision throughout the Bible. However, one's ability to appropriate the benefits of His promises is tied to one's belief and acts of faith. True biblical faith believes and acts with confidence upon that which God has promised. I've heard it said, "Faith isn't a leap into the dark but a step into the light!"

There are many factors that affect faith, for example: 1) your theology 2) your experience 3) and the testimonies of others. Replacing these factors with God's truth builds faith. Your experience, positive or negative, doesn't determine the truth of God's nature and character nor the truth of His Word. Likewise, your church background or theological understanding must align with the truth of God's Word. Otherwise, your faith could be adversely affected.

Faith at its base level is simply trusting God. He honors faith, and it pleases Him. The writer of Hebrews states this truth:

> *It's impossible to please God without faith because the one who draws near to God must believe that he exists and that he rewards people who try to find him.* (Heb. 11:6 CEB)

The Scripture calls one to believe God exists and to trust that He rewards those who seek Him. Miraculously, God promises to respond to them. Faith moves God's heart, causing the release of His grace. God's Word compels us to confidently approach God for grace and faith when we need it.

As I've stated, when we need more faith, we must look to Jesus and spend time at His feet. Real faith comes from Christ, imparted to us by grace. Sometimes faith is weak, but even weak faith is not to be criticized. Sometimes, all the faith you have is enough to cling to Jesus. Nineteenth century pastor Charles Spurgeon said, "Sometimes faith is little more than a simple clinging to Christ in a sense of utter dependence…always cling to what you know…cling to Jesus, for that is faith."[1]

While we want to grow in faith and have the faith from God to move mountains, we also need to be cautious not to condemn ourselves or be critical of others' weak or immature faith. Jesus invites us to live from His faith, faith that comes from God. Only God can give us faith that is confident amid contradiction.

When we have faith from God, we can push aside doubts and fears, and trust Him. Faith from God operating within us, connects us to His kingdom realm and unlocks the resources of heaven—it is the essence of real faith.

The writer of Hebrews says, *"Now faith is the assurance [title deed, confirmation] of things hoped for [divinely guaranteed], and the evidence of things not seen [the conviction of their reality—faith comprehends as fact what cannot be experienced by the physical senses]."* (Heb. 11:1 AMPC)

Faith holds in hope the promise like holding a title deed—such as a car or house title. When you have the deed to a car or house, it's yours. In the same way, faith is your assurance that the promise is yours before the full natural manifestation.

Another metaphor for a hopeful faith is ordering food at a fast food counter. You order the fish tacos, pay for them, are handed a receipt, and wait for them to be made. You have the receipt, the food is already yours, but it's not yet ready. You must wait in expectant hope to see the manifestation of your faith—fish tacos!

Real faith is not merely an intellectual exercise, but a spiritual one. It is primarily in the heart, not in the mind that faith flourishes. Real faith from God is free from the influence of limited natural knowledge. Faith perceives as fact what is not revealed to the natural senses. Faith believes God's promises to make unseen realities available on earth. Faith is forward leaning—it hears, sees, speaks, endures and receives what is promised before it manifests.

Your answers are connected to God through His promises in another realm—a heavenly kingdom where you are seated with Christ. To attempt to have prayer answered, or promises granted, apart from Jesus is unfeasible, He is the originator of your faith. To receive anything in this earthly realm, we must live from our union with Christ and the heavenly realm. This where confident faith is received and developed.

Mountain Moving Faith and Faith from God

Faith to move mountains begins with believing that God hears your prayers. Let's recap what Jesus said about faith that could move mountains.

In Mark 11, after Jesus curses the fig tree and it is discovered the next day withered Jesus responds, *"...Have faith in God! I assure you that whoever says to this mountain, 'Be lifted up and thrown into the sea'—and doesn't waver but believes that what is said will really happen—it will happen."* (Mark 11:22-23 CEB) The phrase, *"have faith in God..."* implies that, with faith, mountains, or incredible situations, will be removed or changed. But where does this faith originate? Is it our faith, faith in God's Word, or is it faith given by God?

To answer these questions, let's beginning by examining the phrase "have faith in God," which is translated from the Greek, *pistis Theos*, or literally in English *faith God*. According to Dr. Charles S. Price, Mark 11:22 can be translated "have faith of God."[2] Charles was known for great faith, but he was also known to discourage faith that was of human effort or desire. He strongly believed that one must have an assurance of faith, and that faith could only come from God.

Nineteenth century scholar Robert Young, translated the Mark 11:22 passage in his Young's Literal Translation (YLT), "... `Have faith of God.`" Dr. Brian Simmons recently translated Mark 11:22 in The Passion Translation (TPT) as, "... *"Let the faith of God be in you!"* Dr. Randy Clark, founder and president of Global Awakening, also believes Mark 11:22 could be translated "faith of God."

Paul, in writing to the Galatians, discusses the "faith of God," or faith that comes from God. Paul writes in Gal. 2:16, *"Knowing that a man is not justified by the works of the law but by faith in Jesus Christ..."* In Gal. 2:16, another translation of "faith in Jesus Christ" would be the "faith of Christ." Young's Literal Translation catches this English nuance of the Greek in this verse, "... *faith of Jesus Christ.*" (Gal. 2:16 YLT) The phrase "faith in Jesus Christ" is translated from the Greek πίστις (*pistis*) Ἰησοῦς (*Iēsous*) or in English simply *faith Jesus*.

A few verses later, Paul writes, *"I have been crucified with Christ; it is no longer I who live, but Christ lives in me; and the life which I now live in the flesh I live by faith in the Son of God, who loved me and gave Himself for me."* (Gal. 2:20) The phrase "faith in the

Son" is translated from the Greek πίστις (*pistis*) υίός (*Huios*) or literally in English *faith Son*. The English word *in* was added by translators of the NKJV, as well as most recent English translations. However, the YLT translation reads, "... *in the faith I live of the Son of God...* "

Galatians 2:16, 20, like Mark 11:22, could be translated "faith of God" or "faith of Christ" or "faith of the Son." Dr. Craig Keener, professor of Biblical Studies at Asbury Theological Seminary agrees that these passages, as well as Mark 11:22, could read "faith of God," "faith of Christ" or "faith of the Son."

Most believe God is all-powerful and able to do anything, they have "faith in God." But to have the "faith of God," or faith that comes from God, is to have the essence of mountain moving faith. You see, faith isn't something we work up, it is a gift from God, imparted by the Spirit. Each of us have received a portion of God's gift of faith to us, "*...God has measured out a portion of faith to each one of you.*" (Rom 12:3 CEB) Notice, it's God who gives the faith, He measures it out. We need to walk in and use the measure of faith that God has given us, without becoming presumptuous in our understanding or even our prayers.

In other words, we may not see answers to prayer (one of many reasons), because our prayers are outside of the will or sovereignty of God. It is important to have God's perspective and faith from God when believing for mountains to be moved. That said, when we genuinely have faith from God, just a tiny mustard seed of it in our hearts, mountains are removed! The principle is to look to Jesus and wait on God for the gift of faith for your situation.

Dr. Price said, "Real faith is of the heart—and only God can put faith in a heart."[3] Just reciting or claiming a verse isn't faith—it is belief. When genuine faith is at work in your heart, you have a knowing, a conviction, it is done. Therefore, understand that faith is an imparted grace from Christ to our hearts. It's not an intellectual understanding, but a revelation to the heart by the grace of God.

In the New Testament (NT), only one other place talks about mountain moving faith, which Paul mentions, *"And though I have the gift of prophecy, and understand all mysteries and all knowledge, and though I have all faith, so that I could remove mountains, but have not love, I am nothing."* (1 Cor. 13:2) Therefore, it could be argued that if you exercise the gifts of the Spirit (1 Cor 12) through the motivation of love, it relates to the gift of faith, which is one of the nine gifts mentioned in the 1 Cor. 12 passage. Paul writes, *"The same Spirit gives great faith to another, and to someone else the one Spirit gives the gift of healing."* (1 Cor. 12:9 NLT)

Do you see the similarity to Mark 11:22, "have faith in God?" The Spirit gives great faith, or a gift of faith, which is the faith from God. To see difficult situations change, we need to ask God for a gift of faith. The gift of faith is mountain moving faith and comes from God. God is the source of mountain moving faith.

Dr. Price balanced this truth, "All things are possible to them that believe. But it is important what you believe. To believe that you, apart from grace and divine imparting, are the possessor of a power that can remove mountains is dangerous indeed. I know many who have believed that way and tried to exercise such power, but sorrow was their lot instead of joy."[4]

What did he mean by "sorrow was their lot instead of joy?" He is referring to sincere people, who were trying to believe, trying to move mountains in their lives or for others, but they did not possess the gift of faith or faith from God in that moment for that situation. In their sincere effort to realize a miracle, for themselves or others, they were disappointed with unanswered prayer.

Dr. Paul King, pastor and author states concerning failures and limitations of faith, "Faith has not been imparted by God. Trusting in one's own faith or another's faith or word, rather than receiving assurance or a touch from God, can also be a reason for unanswered prayer."[5] He further adds that classic faith teachers cautioned against acting on others' faith or word or trying to prove faith.

Faith can be received only as it is imparted to the heart, by God himself. Either you have faith, or you do not. Yes, you can partner with the Holy Spirit to grow your faith, but genuine mountain moving faith comes from God as a gift. Be careful of presumption or simply declaring a Scripture apart from an assurance by the Spirit that the answer is yours—real faith is rooted in faith given by God!

If you lack faith, or are believing for a miracle, ask God for faith without doubt. Wait upon Him and get His assurance and perspective, your faith will increase, and you will remain confident in Him.

John writes, *"And this is the victory that has overcome the world— our faith."* (1 John 5:4b) Faith from God, active in the heart of a believer, is a faith that overcomes the world (world systems and evil). It is a faith that perseveres no matter how dark it is, no matter what the challenge may be, and is confident that God will move the mountain.

Chapter Five

Characteristics of Faith

"...each has been given a measure of faith." Rom. 12:3

"In the face of Jesus, the light which leads to 'the full assurance of faith' is always found. To gaze upon His face, to sit still at His feet that the light of His love may shine upon the soul is a sure way of obtaining a strong faith." Andrew Murray

Have you ever been to the Grand Canyon in Arizona? If you haven't, I encourage you to make the trip. It is a natural wonder to behold. If you have gone, you experienced something beautiful and breathtaking. You viewed the vastness of this magnificent canyon in its vibrant colors and imagery that pictures can't fully represent. Think for a moment as you stood there overlooking the canyon. What did you see? How did objects appear in the distance of the canyon? What did you feel as you gazed into the canyon? The vastness of the canyon impacts not only one's senses, but one's perspective on God's creation.

Now, think for a moment about faith. Did it ever occur to you that faith *sees*? Faith sees in the distance, beyond the expanse of the "canyons" in front of us, to apprehend the promises of God. The eyes of faith grasp the enormity of what God is revealing and offering to us. Faith believes that all things are possible with God! In fact, I believe for some of you reading this, God is offering you something, inviting you into something, which is just on the other side of the "canyon" in front of you. However, it will take faith to cross and receive the inheritance of the promise.

God is the Originator of Faith

When I want faith, I must seek Jesus, He is the originator and perfecter of our faith. Real faith is faith that comes from Christ, imparted to us by the Spirit. As I shared in the previous chapter, Jesus instructed us to have faith that comes from God, "... *Have faith of God.*" (Mark 11:22 YLT) Faith isn't something we merely develop by our own effort, yet we can position ourselves for increase. All faith originates with God, imparted by the Spirit. Genuine "mountain-moving" faith God imparts.

Each of us has received a portion of God's faith we are responsible to cultivate in our lives. God gives us a portion of faith to initially believe, and then God allows us time to mature as we follow Him. Therefore, faith is both a gift of God and a fruit of the Spirit—all faith originates with God. If you want more faith, look to Jesus and ask. In addition, position yourself by reading God's Word, pray, worship, obey, and serve Jesus as

He leads. As you partner with the Holy Spirit, your faith will increase. Faith is both a gift and a fruit that begins with God's deposit in our lives.

Characteristics of Faith

God communicates to us in many ways. I refer to it as the "language of the Spirit." We see many examples throughout the Bible of God communicating to humanity through spoken words, impressions, visions, dreams, and circumstances.

Most of the time when someone says they "hear" God, it isn't the audible voice of God. Rather, it is a gentle impression to one's spirit by the Holy Spirit. It could be a Bible verse or verses, a few words, thoughts, pictures, or dreams. God may even send an angel. We shouldn't be surprised by this since the Bible is full of examples of God communicating through heavenly messengers.

Jesus said plainly that His sheep hear His voice and they listen and follow Him (John 10:1–15). Intrinsic to following Christ is the ability to know and understand His voice. While many who follow Christ struggle to discern God's voice, the reality is Jesus wants to help you cultivate the ability to know His voice—or to know the language of the Spirit.

Why is this so important? Faith flourishes when we are confident in what we have heard or seen from God. To live the abundant life God intended for you, learning to recognize His voice is foundational for confident faith. When you know you have heard from God, your actions will demonstrate faith. Your prayer life will transform, as you learn to agree with the revealed will of God—praying from heaven's perspective toward our earthly realm.

You can try and generate faith, but that's not faith from God, that's human effort. Sure, you can posture yourself to grow in faith with the deposit He gives, and each of us should do so, but whether faith comes as a gift or develops in our lives as an aspect of the fruit of the Spirit, it all comes from God. Every mountain that we see moved, we may think it's our faith, but in truth, it's faith from God at work in us.

Often, what we call faith is trust. We can trust in God's promises but not have the faith to act upon them. Trust is part of the assurance of the mind, but true faith is an assurance of the heart. For example, someone can say, "I believe Jesus can save me, but I'm not ready to follow Him." Faith to believe in Jesus comes from God, for His Spirit is at work drawing us to Him. This person trusts in God's promise of salvation but has not yet moved into faith to claim their new inheritance.

Jesus, who is the author and finisher of your faith, wants you to be a dynamic, faith-filled believer who is confident through every circumstance and season of your life. When we understand the depth of our relationship with Him, the authority He has given, and how often He communicates to build our faith, we begin to live as overcomers. Victorious overcomers cause the powers of darkness to tremble and flee—they advance God's kingdom triumphantly.

Faith leans into the promises of God with expectation of the fulfillment. Faith hears, sees, speaks, endures, and receives what is promised before the manifestation. Let's exam these spiritual characteristics of faith that are similar to our five natural senses.

Faith Hears

A verse most of us are familiar with is Romans 10:17, *"So then faith comes by hearing, and hearing by the word of God."* Paul makes a direct link between hearing God and faith. When we have heard what God is saying, faith increases. *Word* used in this verse translates from the Greek word *rhēma*. To understand *rhēma* better, let's examine an account in Luke with the birth of Jesus.

Perhaps you remember the story. The shepherds are out in their fields at night when God's angel appears and announces to them the great news of the Messiah's birth. After the angelic pronouncement, they say to each other, *"let's go see this thing..."* (Luke 2:15). See this thing—what? Were they doubters of what the angel just declared to them? The English word *thing* in this verse is translated from the word *rhēma*.

The Passion Translation says of this verse, *"Let's go! Let's hurry and find this Word that is born in Bethlehem and see for ourselves what the Lord has revealed to us."* (Luke 2:15 TPT) Let's hurry and find this *Word*, (also translated from *rhēma*) that is born to us. The Greek word *rhēma* means, "that which is said or spoken,[1] an active word,[2] a happening to which one may refer—'matter, thing, event.'[3] *Rhēma* then is "an active word, that causes a manifestation or event."

In Rom. 10:17 in The Passion Translation says, *"Faith, then, is birthed in a heart that responds to God's anointed utterance of the Anointed One."* Faith is birthed in the heart that responds to God's anointed utterance, or to the word spoken in season by Jesus! For me, God's word, or anointed utterance, comes in subtle impressions to my spirit. The Holy Spirit gently speaks and invites me to "believe what God is offering." As I choose to respond, grace is imparted to me to believe and act upon the uttered word.

The English word *faith* in Romans 10:17 is from the Greek word *pistis* meaning, "to believe to the extent of complete trust and reliance—'to believe in, to have confidence in, to have faith in, to trust, faith, trust.'"[4] But how does this complete trust, reliance and confidence develop in someone? It develops by receiving the communicated, active word of God. Therefore faith, or confident reliance and trust, develops from a God-inspired active word that is received, believed, and acted upon.

Let's look at Abraham and Sarah, and what Paul wrote about their faith in his letter to the Romans:

> "[17] *As it is written: I have appointed you to be the father of many nations. So Abraham is our father in the eyes of God in whom he had faith, the God who gives life to the dead and calls things that don't exist into existence.* [18] *When it was beyond hope, he had faith in the hope that he would become the father of many nations, in keeping with the promise God spoke to him: That's how many descendants you will have.* [19] *Without losing faith, Abraham, who was nearly 100 years old, took into account his own body, which was as good as dead, and Sarah's womb, which was dead.* [20] *He didn't hesitate with a lack of faith in God's promise, but he grew strong in faith and gave glory to God.* [21] *He was fully convinced that God was able to do what he promised.*" (Rom. 4:17–21 CEB)

The NKJV of verse 20 translates, "[20] *He did not waver at the promise of God through unbelief, but was strengthened in faith, giving glory to God.*" The English word waver in this translation is from the

Greek word *diakrinō*, which has two meanings, 1) to judge thoroughly or decide between two opinions 2) denotes a conflict within oneself, to hesitate, have misgivings, to doubt or waver between hope and fear.[5]

We could paraphrase what Paul wrote by saying Abraham didn't fluctuate between two opinions. He didn't hesitate, doubt, or waver between hope and unbelief. Rather, during years of waiting for the promise of Isaac, Abraham's faith grew stronger. Keep in mind that Abraham and Sarah weren't perfect; on more than one occasion they deviated from God's perfect will. Yet, the Holy Spirit through Paul indicates that Abraham remained faithful to what God promised. Why?

I believe the answer is discovered in God's nature and in the power of the promise. God spoke a living word to Abraham. The word was active in his heart creating faith to believe the promise spoken to him. Abraham grew strong in faith because of the power of God and the power of the promise.

Abraham received this promise of being the father of many nations in small seed form but cultivated it within his heart. His faith grew and the promise became reality. Keep in mind that Abraham and Sarah weren't perfect in faith. In fact, at one point they laughed at God's promise of the son Isaac (Gen 17–18). But God, who can bring life to that which is dead, looked past the "deadness" of their circumstance and brought forth life. Faith became active in Abraham's heart because of the promise spoken to him. Faith came by hearing, and hearing by the word of God.

God's word or promise is like a seed. Seeds, although small, have life in them. You could say "there is power and life in the seed." And so, it is with God's Word. His Word is living and active; there is life and power in it (Heb. 4:12).

When God's Word is received in a heart that is fertile, it takes root, grows to maturity and produces a harvest (Mark 4:1-20). But doubt and unbelief are like rocky, unfertile soil. It is difficult for seed, except for weeds, to take root easily in rocky, unfertile soil. But in good soil, a crop can be expected.

James has some thoughts about faith and doubt:

> *⁵ If any of you lacks wisdom, let him ask of God, who gives to all liberally and without reproach, and it will be given to him. ⁶ But let him ask in faith, with no doubting, for he who doubts is like a wave of the sea driven and tossed by the wind. ⁷ For let not that man suppose that he will receive anything from the Lord; ⁸ he is a double-minded man, unstable in all his ways.* (James 1:5-8)

Doubting in verse 6 is also from the Greek word *diakrinō*. James, like Paul, states that to receive anything from God, our prayer must be asked in faith without wavering between hope and unbelief. Otherwise it's a faith as unpredictable as a wave driven by the wind.

By the way, if you've ever observed a storm-tossed lake or ocean, with high waves driven by the wind, I'm sure you would agree it's not a safe place to be. Wavering between faith and unbelief isn't safe, it's as dangerous as high waves on a lake or ocean. It can be deadly!

On different occasions, God has spoken to me to purchase sound equipment for our church. Sometimes, it made no sense in the natural. The first such occurrence was purchasing a Sony Cassette and CD Player before we planted our church in Tucson. He simply said, "I want you to go and buy a cassette and CD Player, you're going to need it for the work that I have for you in this city."

We hadn't been in town a month, and we only had about $100 in our ministry account. But God was starting to direct us toward church planting, and it began over several years of incremental steps of faith and obedience. Once I "heard the word," faith was imparted to me to act. I went and bought a Sony player, costing about $60, and waited on God. Within a year we were planting a church and that piece of equipment was used significantly for the first few years. It now sits in my home office as a memorial stone to the faithfulness of God!

Eighteen years later, I marvel at the magnitude and quality of sound equipment we have in our church sanctuary today, and I stand in awe of God. But I first had to respond to a simple word, at a moment it didn't make sense to my natural mind. God could see a church established before we held a single service. He just needed me to take the steps of faith to make it a reality.

Continue to Hear His Voice
Abraham and Sarah were promised a son, and twenty-five years later the son of promise, Isaac, was born. Sometime later, God directs Abraham to offer Isaac on Mt. Moriah as a sacrifice. Abraham obeys God. Upon their arrival, he prepares an altar, binds his son, and lifts his arm to sacrifice his son! Just then, God sends an angel who declares, "Spare your son!" Ultimately, God provides a ram in the thicket for Abraham to sacrifice. To say that Abraham was tested is an understatement!

Here's the point: Abraham "heard God," but as he obeyed, he had to "hear God." He acted on what God said, but future fulfillment of promise in Isaac required Abraham to hear presently what God was communicating. Faith comes from hearing God's anointed utterance—now.

Regarding prophecy or words God has spoken to you, understand that while yesterday's word is important, and key prophecies can be directive over a lifetime, you must also learn to hear presently as you follow the Spirit. There are days and seasons where you may not hear a word from God, during those times, rest in what God has said and focus on His presence and peace.

Don't Be Offended at God!
God communicates or acts in ways that can offend our natural minds. To recognize what God is communicating and doing, we must be a people of His Spirit and Word. When Jesus was born in a humble stable, many in Israel didn't recognize the grace of God at work in their midst. The religious leaders and most of the people didn't recognize the Messiah walking among them performing miracles, healing the sick, casting out demons, and raising the dead. Why? They didn't recognize the Spirit upon His words and actions.

To illustrate this, let me share a story from a friend, Steve Swanson, an itinerate worship minister. Steve was at our church one Sunday and heard me teach on the power of communion. He later shared the following story with me, illustrating both the importance of communion and recognizing what the Spirit of God is revealing and doing presently:

"I was at a conference in Chicago a few years ago. Harold and Kaye Beyer were guest speakers. Harold, who has since passed, was a precious man around eighty years of age at the time of the conference. Harold was having manna supernaturally appear in his meetings! During this conference, his Bible was full of manna. Harold decided to take communion at the end of the meeting with the manna that supernaturally appeared. Seven-hundred people, including myself, lined up to take communion. I was near the end of the line of people when the manna ran out.

Harold said a precious prayer, "Oh Lord if You could please send some more manna so everyone could receive communion!" Suddenly, more than enough manna again appeared! My knee was swollen and inflamed at the time and I couldn't bend it because of pain. I was able to receive the manna during this communion service and immediately I could feel the pain leave and the swelling in my knee go down. I could feel heat as the pain left, and mobility returned—there is healing in communion—and supernatural manna doesn't hurt either! I was blown away by the goodness of God!"

Steve received a healing because he focused on Jesus, the substance and person of communion. The supernatural sign (manna) simply encouraged his faith. He approached God with childlike faith, knowing that healing was available through Christ and the sacrament of communion.

Jesus' words were empowered, but many disciples turned from following Him because they couldn't receive the grace on His words (see John 6). Jesus said to the disciples who continued to follow Him, *"the words that I speak to you are Spirit and they are life."* (John 6:63) Learn to recognize the Spirit upon the words or impressions communicated by the Lord or through others—your faith will increase as you hear what God is saying or doing!

God's promises transcend your perspective and circumstances. Focus your mind on what God has done or is doing. Refuse to entertain thoughts which question God, or His ways—that's unbelief. Faith receives the promise as reality, often before your understanding or senses can fully grasp what God is doing.

Faith Sees

Faith sees through God's eyes and from His perspective. Our perspective, apart from faith from God, is limited in clarity. I happen to be near-sighted and need prescription glasses to see in the distance. If I take off my glasses, everything in the distance appears blurry. Spiritually speaking, without God's "faith glasses," none of us see clearly in the distance.

Remember my Grand Canyon illustration? Without my prescription glasses, everything is blurry in the distance as I look out over the canyon. For many of us, we're trying to see in the distance. God is offering us the unimaginable through His promises, but it is difficult to see without God's "faith glasses."

The story of God showing Abram the promised land illustrates this truth, *"After Lot separated from him, the Lord said to Abram, "From the place where you are standing, look up and gaze to the north, south, east, and west, because all the land that you see I give you and your descendants forever."* (Gen. 13:14–15 CEB)

Abram's nephew, Lot, took what appeared to be the best land. But God showed Abram the land of promise in the distant horizon. Lot couldn't see it, and until God revealed it to Abram, he couldn't see it either. Once God revealed it to Abram, he could "see by faith" what God was offering. Faith was imparted, and Abram could act on what was revealed to him.

Abram was being offered an inheritance for generations. God communicated through sight and vision. But God was revealing more than land. God was revealing to Abram that he would be the "father of many nations." Abram had to see beyond the challenges and contradictory circumstances of life to trust in the promise of his inheritance. And so, it is for you and me. Faith sees in the distance, beyond the distance in front of us, to apprehend the promises of God. The eyes of faith believe that all things are possible with God.

Seeing from God's Perspective
Sometimes our vision is too small or distorted. People "see" themselves through the negativity of the past. It could be failures, wrongs, hurts, offenses, judgments, etc. that rob us from seeing clearly what God is saying "now." Again, for some reading this, I believe God is revealing a broad horizon in front of you, but it takes faith eyes to see it! Ask God for fresh vision, and new clarity to see what He is revealing to you in this season. Perhaps like Abram, you are about to receive a tremendous promise and breakthrough!

The Holy Spirit has been poured out upon all flesh. Jesus, the light of the world, shines upon the heart of everyone. Yet, most are unaware of His light and presence—they are unable to "see." It takes faith to see God amidst the contradiction and chaos surrounding us. For many, fear hinders God's promises that are close. The kingdom of heaven is at hand—it is very near. Many are unable to recognize what God is doing in plain view.

In 2 Kings 6:8–23, we read of Elisha and the invisible army of God surrounding him. It provides a dramatic illustration of the power of spiritual sight from God's perspective.

> *[15] Elisha's servant got up early and went out. He saw an army with horses and chariots surrounding the city. His servant said to Elisha, "Oh, no! Master, what will we do?" [16] "Don't be afraid," Elisha said, "because there are more of us than there are of them." [17] Then Elisha prayed, "Lord, please open his eyes that he may see." Then the Lord opened the servant's eyes, and he saw that the mountain was full of horses and fiery chariots surrounding Elisha.* (2 Kings 6:15–17 CEB)

Once Elisha prayed, his servant could see the angelic host surrounding them. Your natural circumstances may seem daunting, but the angelic host enveloping you are very real. They are ministering spirits, sent to help and protect us (Heb. 1:14). Elisha's servant could not spiritually see the reality surrounding him and Elisha. Fear brought the servant into confusion and spiritual blindness to the truth of the situation. Fear denies your spiritual eyes the opportunity to see what is real.

You may never see angels or the invisible hand of God in your situation but know that God is always with you. He will never leave you nor forsake you, not for the slightest moment.

The Eyes of Your Heart Enlightened
Do you remember the story of the apostle Thomas, known by many as "Doubting Thomas?" Thomas, like most of us, wanted

to see to believe. Jesus had risen from the dead and began to appear in His glorified body to some of the disciples (John 20). They told Thomas, "*We have seen the Lord!*" *So he said to them, "Unless I see in His hands the print of the nails, and put my finger into the print of the nails, and put my hand into His side, I will not believe."* (John 20:24–25)

After eight anxious and agonizing days for Thomas (doubt creates anxiety and negativity, it is fear-based instead of faith-based), Jesus appeared to him and the other disciples. The first thing Jesus said to the group was, "*Peace to you.*" Proclaiming peace over those who struggle with doubt and fear provides a foundation for faith to be established.

Jesus then said to Thomas, *"27Put your finger here. Look at my hands. Put your hand into my side. No more disbelief. Believe!" 28Thomas responded to Jesus, "My Lord and my God!" 29Jesus replied, "Do you believe because you see me? Happy are those who don't see and yet believe."* (John 20:27–29 CEB)

Thomas saw and believed, but Jesus states that you and I are blessed or happy when we believe even though we do not see Him. As a follower of Christ, this must be your position. You may never see Jesus, but you should believe His Word and the testimony of others. You know He is alive through your faith and by the Holy Spirit living in you. After experiencing your new birth in Christ, the Holy Spirit empowers you to have eyes of faith to see. These are not just metaphorical "faith eyes," but the capacity to receive revelation from God that may enable you to see into unseen spiritual realms.

In Ephesians, Paul prayed for believers to have a spirit of wisdom and revelation, and for the eyes of their hearts to be illuminated to the truth of who Christ is and what He has accomplished:

> *¹⁷ ...that the God of our Lord Jesus Christ, the Father of glory, may give to you a spirit of wisdom and of revelation in the knowledge of Him. ¹⁸ I pray that the eyes of your heart may be enlightened, so that you will know what is the hope of His calling, what are the riches of the glory of His inheritance in the saints.* (Eph. 1:17–18 NASB)

Have you ever considered that your heart has eyes? When Paul refers to your heart, he is not referring to the beating muscle tissue in your chest but the center of your spiritual being that knows and relates to God. Through faith in Christ, you have been given spiritual eyes to see, have the capacity to know Jesus intimately, and can understand revelation from God. What you experience with your natural senses is real, but the unseen spiritual world around you is just as real—even more than that, it is eternal. What you see with the eyes of your heart is as real to you as what you see with your natural eyes.

The apostle Paul was guided daily by the Holy Spirit, who at times communicated with Paul through visions. On two occasions, the Holy Spirit stopped Paul and his team from traveling into other regions. He was given a "vision in the night" of a man from Macedonia asking him and his team to come and help them. We read in Acts:

> *⁶ Next Paul and Silas traveled through the area of Phrygia and Galatia, because the Holy Spirit had prevented them from preaching the word in the province of Asia at that time. ⁷ Then*

coming to the borders of Mysia, they headed north for the province of Bithynia, but again the Spirit of Jesus did not allow them to go there. ⁸ So instead, they went on through Mysia to the seaport of Troas. ⁹ That night Paul had a vision: A man from Macedonia in northern Greece was standing there, pleading with him, "Come over to Macedonia and help us!" ¹⁰ So we decided to leave for Macedonia at once, having concluded that God was calling us to preach the Good News there. (Acts 16:6–10 NLT)

This simple vision enabled Paul to see and understand what God was communicating. It empowered him to believe in God's direction and plan. Paul's faith was strengthened after receiving God's vision, and based on the revelation, he was confident about his new assignment. As followers of Christ, God wants to do the same for you and I—communicate clearly to us through visionary encounters.

God promised us through Jeremiah, *"Call to me and I will answer and reveal to you wondrous secrets that you haven't known."* (Jer. 33:3 CEB) And in Deuteronomy, God declares, *"The secret things belong to the LORD our God, but those things which are revealed belong to us and to our children forever, that we may do all the words of this law."* (Deut. 29:29)

When was the last time you asked God to reveal His wondrous secrets and strategies to you? God wants to reveal His secrets to His people because revelation imparts faith to the one who sees and hears. Expect to see and understand what God wants to reveal to you and to the Church in this hour!

The ancient prophets were often called seers, who could "see" prophetically into what God was revealing. This practice of seeing or hearing revelation is still available today. Those that have trained their spiritual senses to understand the language of the Holy Spirit value the impressions they receive.

Learning how God communicates to you is important. It is an awareness that develops over time as you walk with God. Faith grows by understanding what God is communicating and trusting it will come to pass. While you may never see Jesus, if you believe then you can see—you have faith eyes.

I once heard this statement, "if you can see it, you can have it." I have found this to be true with God's revealed will. Visualization is powerful, and God often deposits a gift of faith through what is revealed to you. Once you see or perceive what God desires for you to comprehend, your faith and trust for the desired outcome will grow.

Real faith is anchored in your new life in Christ and union with Him through the Holy Spirit. This intimacy empowers you to come with confidence and boldness before God and ask in faith for the things you need. Faith-filled vision comprehends the nature and ascension glory of Jesus.

Your prophetic vision and understanding of Christ will release all other vision, because He is the author of your faith. It grows your understanding of who you are in Him. As you are anchored in your union with Christ, you are united with Him in His victory and glory. Perceiving God as He is enables you to be changed into His image. As His follower you share His new life and nature (2 Pet. 1:4). Your revelatory experience in Christ empowers you to live the words He gives you with confidence. Vision captivates, empowers, and moves you to action.

Faith Speaks

Faith speaks and proclaims what we believe. Confessing God's truths, builds structure in the Spirit that affects our lives. Faith says, "I am going to look through the darkness of the situation and declare what God says." Faith is fueled by hope.

Zerubbabel was responsible for rebuilding the temple and was instructed to trust God's power, not the mere resources of man to accomplish the task. *"Not by might nor by power, but by My Spirit, says the Lord..."* (Zech. 4:6). The temple reconstruction stalled for about sixteen years as the people gave into opposition, discouragement, and apathy (Ezra 5:1–2).

But, the prophet Zechariah declares, *"Who are you, O great mountain? Before Zerubbabel you shall become a plain! And he shall bring forth the capstone with shouts of Grace, grace to it!"* (Zech. 4:7) All of the opposition, discouragement, and lack of resources represented a "mountain" that stood in the way. What did the prophet do? He began to speak and declare, by faith, what God would do. After the prophet spoke, the people rose to complete the rebuilding of the temple. Zechariah declared God's will by faith, which caused a "shift" in the minds and hearts of the people.

Remember the words of Jesus in Mark regarding declarative faith:

> [22] *Jesus responded to them, "Have faith in God!* [23] *I assure you that whoever says to this mountain, 'Be lifted up and thrown into the sea'—and doesn't waver but believes that what is said will really happen—it will happen.* [24] *Therefore I say to you, whatever you pray and ask for, believe that you will receive it, and it will be so for you.* (Mark 11:22–24 CEB)

When you have God's imparted faith, you begin to pray and speak with a confidence that the promise is received and is on its way! Jesus also said in Matthew's gospel, *"The mouth speaks out of that which fills the heart."* (Matt. 12:34b NASB) When God's truth and assurance fills your heart, declaring what He has given faith for becomes normal for the confident follower of Christ. When we confess God's truths, a framework of faith is established for God to bring to pass the promise.

It is God who gives life to the dead and calls things into being that were nonexistent. Imagine the conversations Abraham and Sarah must have had! They initially laughed at God's promise of a son in a year (Gen. 17–18). They had waited for twenty-four years to see God's promise fulfilled, and hope had faded. But somewhere between the laughter and God's promise, faith gripped them, and I believe they "spoke God's promise" to each other! The result is that a year later, as God promised, Isaac was born, whose name means laughter!

Deaf Ears Opened!
I was in meetings in Brazil a few years ago with a team from Global Awakening. One of the team members had a word of knowledge about a "deaf right ear." They simply spoke the word out, and it was translated and spoken in Portuguese to the crowd. It turns out, there was a young man present in the meeting who was deaf in both ears since birth. When the word was "spoken" over the airwaves, God did a miracle and his right ear opened!

Keep in mind he couldn't hear the word spoken; both of his ears were deaf. But the faith-filled word created a framework for God to bring about a miracle. He was brought forward by a family member to testify to what God did, and after more prayer the left deaf ear was also opened and healed—everyone praised God for His greatness and love that night! By faith, the word of knowledge was spoken, and God worked a miracle. Faith speaks, and often our minds can't comprehend what God is about to do!

Faith Endures

Patient endurance is needed to run your race of faith. The writer of Hebrews states, *"through faith and patience we inherit the promises."* (Heb. 6:12) Patience undergirds our faith and helps us to endure. Faith is an expectant anticipation of the reality of the promise before the manifestation appears. It causes us to act upon God's revealed truth with an assurance of the answer. Patience undergirds our faith and helps us to endure. Faith is proactive, not passive and trusts in God completely.

We look to Jesus, who is our example and the one working in us to mature our faith. We remain in hope because He is faithful to complete in you that which began at conversion. Notice in this verse that negative thinking and laziness hinder us from inheriting God's promises.

A few chapters later in Hebrews, we are admonished to patiently endure, *"*[35]* So do not throw away this confident trust in the Lord. Remember the great reward it brings you!* [36] *Patient endurance is what you need now, so that you will continue to do God's will. Then you will receive all that he has promised."* (Heb. 10:35–36 NLT)

The writer of Hebrews was specifically encouraging many in the early church suffering horrific persecution and martyrdom. However, the principles mentioned in Hebrews 10 and 11:30–40 are applicable for us today.

Salvation is a gift; it's God's grace. Grace then bids you to go further, to become more like Christ (Rom. 8:29), and to do the greater works of Jesus (John 14:12). If you become spiritually lazy or lose the "edge" by drawing back from pursuing God, your spiritual endurance will falter, and you will no longer look for bigger "mountains." You were created for victory, not mediocrity! Victory requires faith to overcome.

Lastly, God's gift of faith in you overcomes the evil in our world. *"And this is the victory that has overcome the world—our faith."* (1 John 5:4b) God's faith, active in the heart of a believer, is a faith that overcomes the world—world systems and evil. It is a faith that perseveres no matter how dark it is and no matter what the challenge may be. It is a faith that is confident God will move the mountain.

As I've shared, Jesus is the founder and perfecter of our faith. Let's examine Hebrews 12:1–2 more closely:

> *[1] Therefore, since we are surrounded by such a huge crowd of witnesses to the life of faith, let us strip off every weight that slows us down, especially the sin that so easily trips us up. And let us run with endurance the race God has set before us. [2] We do this by keeping our eyes on Jesus, the champion who initiates and perfects our faith. Because of the joy awaiting him, he endured the cross, disregarding its shame. Now he is seated in the place of honor beside God's throne.* (Heb. 12:1–2 NLT)

Where is Jesus now? He is victorious and ascended on high, seated at the right hand of the Father. Paul writes in Eph. 2:6 that we are *"seated together with him in heavenly realms."* It's a scandalous grace! Yes, you and I, as imperfect as we are, have been united with Christ, positioned in Him, far above all powers and principalities. The devil is under our feet because he is underneath the feet of Jesus our champion.

We live and move and have our being in Jesus, and we look to Him knowing that He is perfecting our faith. The more aware we are of our position in Christ, the more we can live from the divine union of both the Word and the Spirit. The Spirit takes the written word and makes it come alive because we serve the living Word—Jesus! The eternal word, Jesus, came from heaven, born of human flesh, and His words are Spirit and life. Whether from the written Word or His voice to us, as we learn to recognize what His Spirit is speaking to us, our faith grows. There is tremendous faith in this state—it is the faith of Christ!

We look to Jesus for inspiration as we run the race of faith, and we anticipate His grace is perfecting or maturing our faith. As we yield to the Holy Spirit, we are being transformed into His likeness and we participate in His victory. We too are becoming champions of faith!

The NKJV of Hebrews 12:2 states, *"looking unto Jesus, the author and finisher of our faith..."* The phrase "looking unto" is translated from the Greek word *aphoraō*, which means to "look away from all others and to fix attention on."[6] We are to look away from all distractions and look with singular focus upon Jesus. It is then that our vision and perspective change. As we look into His eyes, His heart, and His character, we begin to see in the realm of the Spirit that takes us beyond a mere earthy understanding of what real faith is.

Some have gone to death as martyrs, because they remained steadfast in faith as the eyes of their heart focused on

Jesus (Heb. 11:30–40). This may be hard for many in twenty first century western culture to fully grasp. However, there are times where even the promises or prophetic words you are holding onto may not be fulfilled, as you understand, in your life. But there is a greater reality—it's the resurrection and the eternal hope of the heavenly Jerusalem with God!

Therefore, remain confident in God, knowing He cares for you always. As Paul wrote, nothing can separate you from His love (Rom. 8:37-39). Your faith isn't just a bridge over troubled waters, your faith sustains you through the troubled waters. Often, we are looking for ways to get over the difficulties. Sometimes the very sufferings and trials we experience are perfecting our faith. Just one glance from Jesus' eye, just one word from Him, and my perspective changes, hope arises, and faith lays hold of His promise!

Grace and faith are inseparably linked. *"For by grace you have been saved through faith, and that not of yourselves; it is the gift of God."* (Eph. 2:8) God's gift of grace to us is reconciliation through Jesus. But as I mentioned earlier, God also gives us a measure of faith to even believe in God's gift of eternal life. We can't earn His grace; it is freely given. Similarly, we can't earn faith; He gives it freely. We have a responsibility to steward the faith given to us, but it is both God's empowering grace and God's gift of faith at work in you! You can't earn your way to grace or faith—you can, however, posture yourself to grow in grace and faith.

God often imparts faith to us when we least deserve it. This is an aspect of his grace. But this grace is more than just your conversion experience. God imparts faith when you and I need it most and least deserve it. The gift of faith causes mountains to move and prayers to be answered, by His grace!

Faith Receives

Faith receives the reality of the promise before the manifestation occurs in the natural realm. The eye of faith observes the unseen eternal realm, and faith enables you to know that those unseen realities and fulfilled promises are real, that they have substance. Faith is forward leaning; it receives what is promised before the manifestation. There is a tangible nature to faith. When you have God's gift of faith regarding a promise or a matter, you know that you have received it.

Faith believes the promise is fulfilled through hope. It is an expectant anticipation of the reality of the promise before the manifestation appears. A gift of faith causes a person to act upon God's revealed truth with an assurance of the answer. It comprehends spiritual promises as facts, even when they are contrary to our five senses or natural understanding of circumstances.

Be careful of human reasoning; it is often blind to God's perspective on His promise to you. The writer of Proverbs underscores this principle, *"⁵ Trust in the LORD with all your heart; do not depend on your own understanding. ⁶ Seek his will in all you do, and he will show you which path to take."* (Prov. 3:5–6 NLT)

In 2004, after receiving specific words and visions to purchase our church property, David, one of our elders, had a vision. He saw a young man doing the triple-jump, and event in track and field where the person runs down a track runway, first does a "hop," followed by a "skip," and then a final "jump" to complete the event. The Lord spoke to him, "Purchasing the church property was the "hop," then you will "skip" and build another sanctuary on this property (which we did in 2010–11), and then you will "jump" to a different location and larger piece of property and building."

In faith, we can receive God's "title deed" of the promise before the final "jump" and manifestation. Purchasing the property was the "hop," or phase one. Building the new sanctuary was the "skip," or phase two. The fact that phase one and two have occurred, deepens our faith that God will bring to pass the "jump" or phase three of all that He has promised the church regarding property. His promise transcends our current perspective and circumstances.

Focus your mind on what God has done or is doing. Refuse to entertain thoughts and critical reasoning that questions God—that's unbelief. Faith receives the promise as reality, often before your understanding or senses can fully grasp what God is doing. When you have faith from God active within, you pray with confidence and assurance you have received what you pray and believe for, despite what you see in the natural. *"Therefore I tell you, whatever you ask for in prayer, believe that you have received it, and it will be yours."* (Mark 11:24)

Chapter Six

Prevailing Faith & Prayer

"If you can believe, all things are possible to him who believes." Mark 9:23

"Perhaps one of the most common ways people's faith is weakened is by assuming it is not God's will to answer their prayers." Gordon Lindsay

Have you ever considered that God gives faith to prevail in prayer? Faith, like any spiritual gift, originates from God. He empowers you through grace to believe and to persevere in faith and prayer. God expects you to utilize the faith you receive; consequently, as you continue to yield to the Holy Spirit, God increases your capacity to operate in more faith.

A few years ago, I was ministering at a church in Brazil and observed firsthand the power of prevailing faith and prayer. The church was in a poor area of the city in a storefront, but the people were rich in faith. When our team arrived at this church, I could hear the intercessors loudly praying in a back room. The pastor asked me if I wanted to join them in prayer before the service started and I said, "Yes!" I love being in prayer meetings where faith and expectation are at work.

As soon as I walked into the prayer room, I could feel the presence of God in a tangible way. These Brazilian believers were praying for souls to be saved, for healings to occur, and for God to do miracles in their midst. I knew God was going to move powerfully in the meeting that night.

After I finished speaking the message, I gave a few words of knowledge about conditions God wanted to heal. One of the words was for a "deaf left ear." A few minutes later, a woman came forward talking to the translator in Portuguese and pointing to her left ear. The woman was deaf in her left ear, but God miraculously opened it after the word of knowledge was given. In addition, she gave her life to Christ that night! She had never been in a church before but was walking by and "felt" that she should come inside.

I believe it was God's power, at work through the faith and prayer of the intercessory team, that created an atmosphere for the Spirit to draw this woman to the meeting, receive a miracle, and then say yes to Jesus. God is not limited to a small church in Brazil. He is looking for those He can strengthen and empower. We must learn how to prevail in faith and prayer to see the greater breakthroughs He longs to bring. Faith to move mountains begins with believing that God hears your prayers and is ready to answer.

Jesus is the object and source of our faith. We look to Him for inspiration to run our race, and we anticipate His grace to perfect or mature our faith. As we yield to the Holy Spirit, we are transformed into the likeness of Christ and participate in His victory. We too become champions of faith as we grow in grace. As we operate in faith from God, we discover that prayer prevails.

Grace and Faith are Linked

We've been made right with God through His grace, which activates faith within us. We can't earn grace through works, but grace invites us to participate in becoming Christ-like and doing the very works of Jesus. Similarly, we can't earn faith; He gives the increase. Grace entails more than our conversion experience. God's grace and faith imparted to our hearts empower us to live from His victory as overcomers. Furthermore, it fuels prevailing prayer that realizes answers.

We have a responsibility to steward the faith given to us, but it is both God's grace and God's gift of faith at work in us. Through proper response to God and His Word, we posture ourselves to *grow* in grace and faith and operate from His will and purpose.

Prevailing Faith initiates Prevailing Prayer

The Holy Spirit causes faith to enlarge and prayer to be more confident and effective. With God's faith, one should expect challenging situations to change; your prayer life will reflect this. There is a connection between mature faith and effective prayer. Jesus is the source of your faith; He is the greater one within. You are united and filled with Christ by the Spirit. Persevering faith and confident prayer are the result of close relationship to Him. Consider what Jesus said about God abiding in us as we believe:

> [15] *If you love me, obey my commandments.* [16] *And I will ask the Father, and he will give you another Advocate, who will never leave you.* [17] *He is the Holy Spirit, who leads into all truth. The world cannot receive him, because it isn't looking for him and doesn't recognize him. But you know him, because he lives with you now and later will be in you.* [18] *No, I will not abandon you as orphans—I will come to you.* [19] *Soon the world will no longer see me, but you will see me. Since I live, you also will live.* [20] *When I am raised to life again, you will know that I am in my Father, and you are in me, and I am in you.* (John 14:15–20 NLT)

Paul states that the fullness of God is in Christ and we are filled with him, "[9] *All the fullness of deity lives in Christ's body.* [10] *And you have been filled by him, who is the head of every ruler and authority.*" (Col 2:9–10 CEB) Jesus is the fullness of God and the Church is the fullness of Christ. Jesus is in us, and He is the fullness of every spiritual blessing. All that pertains to life and godliness are found in Him. How should this reality affect our faith and prayer?

The fullness of God dwells within us; therefore, we are not trying to reach God "out there" somewhere. Rather, we commune with God spirit to Spirit. God is dwelling in the inner most being of the person who follows Jesus! Prevailing faith and prayer originate from the Holy Spirit within us.

Paul also tells us the Holy Spirit helps our prayer life, *"In the same way the Spirit also helps our weakness; for we do not know how to pray as we should, but the Spirit Himself intercedes for us with groanings too deep for words."* (Rom. 8:26 NASB) There are Spirit-inspired times of prayer that go beyond our words. There are stirrings, groanings within us that God wants to release through prayer.

By telling the disciples to "speak to mountains," Jesus was preparing them for situations where they would need to take His authority in the Spiritual realm (Matt. 28:18-19). We've been given Jesus' authority—the very authority of His name. We are filled with the Holy Spirit who empowers our walk with God, our faith, and our prayer life. When you have God's gift of faith, you begin to pray and speak with a confidence that the promise you're waiting for is received and on its way.

We read in Mark's gospel how the authority of Jesus is questioned, *"²⁷ Then they came again to Jerusalem. And as He was walking in the temple, the chief priests, the scribes, and the elders came to Him. ²⁸ And they said to Him, "By what authority are You doing these things? And who gave You this authority to do these things?"* (Mark 11:27-28) The leaders question Jesus about his authority. A religious spirit was at work trying to weaken the faith and confidence of Jesus. In like manner, a religious spirit will try to convince you that you are "full of yourself," prideful, arrogant, etc. Instead, remind yourself that you are full of Christ, confident in Him not in your abilities. Confidence seems arrogant to a religious mindset.

In Acts 3, a man lame since birth receives a miracle healing through the ministry of Peter and John. They are put in prison by the religious leaders, and the next day they are asked, *"By what power or in what name did you do this?"* (Acts 4:7 CEB) Like they did with Jesus, they question the authority of these disciples, accusing them of heresy to weaken their faith.

All authority belongs to Jesus, and He has commissioned us to go in the authority of His name. To prevail in faith and prayer, we must know our position and authority in Christ and remain confident in Him amidst contradiction. A hopeless world needs a bold church! Stay humble, but remain confident in Christ's authority, promises and Spirit within you—you are praying from His victory and power.

Resurrection Power at Work in You

As a born-again believer in Jesus, His resurrection life resides in you. Within you is a power greater than anything in creation. In fact, it is the same power that overcame death and hell (Rom. 5:17; Eph. 1:18–20). This understanding will build your faith and transform your prayer life. Jesus is the source of your new life of faith and prevailing prayer.

Your prayers are not "feeble attempts" to get God's attention. Rather, your prayers have resurrection life attached to them because Jesus releases His presence and power through you. *"Greater is He who is in you than he who is in the world!"* (1 John 4:4 NASB)

When Carolyn and I were newly married, God began to fast-track us to a deeper understanding of the reality of Christ within us. One day, Carolyn came home from work with excruciating pain in her left ear. I said to her, "Let me pray for your ear," to which she happily agreed. I prayed a short commanding prayer telling the pain to go, for infection to leave, and for the ear to function as normal—in Jesus name. No sooner did I finished praying that she said, "Bob, all the pain is gone!" I was so new to this, I said, "Are you sure?!" She said, "Yes, I'm sure! All the pain is gone, and my ear feels normal!" We both rejoiced and thanked God for her healing. His resurrection life was at work through me, despite my inexperience and weak faith for healing ministry.

God's grace and imparted faith empowers reliance on the resurrection power of Christ within and creates confident prayer. Just as grace and faith are connected, so are faith and prayer. God extends grace to first believe in Christ; then, the Spirit empowers us to be people of faith and prayer.

As Jesus is the originator of our faith, the Holy Spirit, who dwells within us, is the initiator of our prayers (Rom. 8:26–27). Just as we tune a radio to a specific station frequency, we need to recognize and "tune in" to the promptings and leadings of the Spirit to pray more confidently and effectively. God is always communicating with us—learn to recognize how and what the Spirit is saying to be more effective in prayer.

Jesus promised that the fullness of God would dwell in the heart of the one who believes, *"Whoever loves me will keep my word. My Father will love them, and we will come to them and make our home with them."* (John 14:23 CEB) We should be dependent upon Him, not of ourselves. His very resurrection life and power are working in and through us if we believe.

You have been given God's faith, God's Spirit, God's promises, and God's authority. Expect difficult situations to change as you prevail in prayer. When you have God's will on a matter, begin to pray and speak with confidence that the promise is received now and is on its way. The fullness of God dwells within you as a follower of Christ. Therefore, as you commune with God from your inner being, spirit to Spirit, God is at work in and through you to answer prayer and change situations.

Jesus Expects You to Petition Him in Prayer

In Matthew's gospel, Jesus teaches the disciples a model for prayer (the Lord's prayer), and begins to give them further principles about petitionary prayer:

> *[7] Ask, and it will be given to you; seek, and you will find; knock, and it will be opened to you. [8] For everyone who asks receives, and he who seeks finds, and to him who knocks it will be opened... [11] How much more will your Father who is in Heaven give good things to those who ask Him!* (Matt. 7:7–8,11)

These verbs: ask, seek, and knock in the Greek mean a continual asking, seeking, and knocking. Pray until you see the answer, or the Holy Spirit indicates to stop praying. Prayer is primarily communion with God. From this place of relationship and communion, God expects us to petition Him in prayer. In other words, don't be afraid to ask God. He already knows what you have need of before you ask of Him, but He invites you and I to petition and partner with Him in prayer. God is a good God! He desires to give all good things to us if we just ask Him.

However, to get assurance that your petitions will be answered, there are conditions that must be met. Here are seven conditions to consider and put into practice for more effective prayer.

You Must Ask in Faith

Simply asking God for things will not assure you of a positive response. *"And all things, whatsoever you ask in prayer, believing, you shall receive."* (Matt. 21:22) *"...but believes that those things he says will be done... whatever things you ask when you pray, believe that you receive them, and you will have them."* (Mark 11:23-24)

This type of faith and belief only come from your relationship with Jesus. If you don't abide in Christ, you simply won't have faith to believe free of doubt.

Again, where is the source of this mountain-moving power? Is it out there somewhere? No, it's Christ within you! To see the exceeding abundance of all that you ask or think, know that it's according to His power at work in you. As I've shared, realize He is working within you to increase your faith as you walk with Him faithfully. If you lack faith, simply ask Jesus for more faith or a gift of faith for your situation.

Ask in the Name of Jesus and the Authority of His Name

In John's gospel, Jesus states, *"[13] And whatever you ask in My name, that I will do, that the Father may be glorified in the Son. [14] If you ask anything in My name, I will do it."* (John 14:13-14) And in the next chapter, Jesus repeats the theme of asking in His name, *"You did not choose Me, but I chose you and appointed you that you should go and bear fruit, and that your fruit should remain, that whatever you ask the Father in My name He may give you."* (John 15:16)

We live from the victory of His ascension and the authority of His name to reign with Him in this life. Consider what Paul wrote about reigning with Christ: *"... those who receive the abundance of grace and of the gift of righteousness will reign in life through the One, Jesus Christ."* (Rom. 5:17 NASB) Don't allow a religious mindset to question your authority in Christ. All authority belongs to Jesus, and He has commissioned you and I to go into the world with the authority of His name (Matt. 28:18-19).

He has "deputized" us, and we are ambassadors of His New Covenant. We are empowered to set captives free and impact the world. To prevail in faith and prayer, we must know our position and authority in Christ and remain confident in Him amidst contrary evidence.

You Must Abide in Christ

You are united with Christ through the power of His resurrection and the indwelling of the Holy Spirit. Learn to live out of this reality and His presence. As you daily abide with Him through prayer, His Word, and your daily walk, His desires become your desires. Your faith will increase, and your prayers will become more confident. *"If you abide in Me, and my words abide in you, you will ask what you desire, and it shall be done for you."* (John 15:7)

Our confidence in life, prayer, and ministry is not in ourselves, but in God. Consider what Paul said to the Corinthians:

> [4] *Such confidence we have through Christ toward God.* [5] *Not that we are adequate in ourselves to consider anything as coming from ourselves, but our adequacy is from God,* [6] *who also made us adequate as servants of a new covenant, not of the letter but of the Spirit; for the letter kills, but the Spirit gives life."* (2 Cor. 3:4–6 NASB)

Prevailing faith and prayer originate from our confidence of God's empowerment and commission worked by the Holy Spirit within us. Through our new life in Christ and the indwelling of the Holy Spirit we have become adequate servants of a New Covenant. We have become empowered ministers of His New Covenant, and effective prayer warriors through the Spirit.

Twentieth century evangelist, Smith Wigglesworth said in his sermon titled *Life in the Spirit*, "...for the life within me is a thousand times bigger than I am on the outside. There must be a tremendous expansion...this life can't be understood in the natural."[1] Jesus must increase! There must be a tremendous expansion of His operative work within and through us.

Just prior to going on a mission trip to Romania in 1993, God spoke a truth to me that I often remind myself and others of. The Lord said to me during prayer that day, "Bob, one man or woman full of faith and the Holy Spirit can shake a nation." I never shook the nation of Romania, but God was teaching me something about faith and life in the Spirit.

Do you remember the story of Stephen in Acts 6–7? He was chosen to help serve the people. It was said, *"And Stephen, full of faith and power, did great wonders and signs among the people."* (Acts 6:8) Stephen understood that abiding with Jesus released His resurrection life through him to impact others. Your assignment is to bring the very resurrection life of Jesus to people and situations that need God's love and power. You are more than an adequate servant of Christ; you are empowered to prevail in prayer and ministry by His faith and Spirit at work in you!

Walk Righteously with God

We read in 1 John, *"21 Dear friends, if we don't feel guilty, we can come to God with bold confidence. 22 And we will receive from him whatever we ask because we obey him and do the things that please him."* (1 John 3:21–22 NLT) Righteous living combined with a clean conscious gives you confidence in prayer. Don't allow the enemy to bring you into compromise and weaken your confidence in Christ and in prayer.

Live in Forgiveness with Others
Unforgiveness is a hinderance to prevailing faith and prayer. Jesus makes this truth clear throughout the gospels, *"²⁵And whenever you stand praying, if you have anything against anyone, forgive him, that your Father in heaven may also forgive you your trespasses. ²⁶But if you do not forgive, neither will your Father in heaven forgive your trespasses."* (Mark 11:25–26)

Jesus, in discussing faith and prayer in the story of the withered fig tree, connected the importance of living in forgiveness to effective prayer. A condition of prevailing prayer is a forgiving spirit. You can't walk in the fullness of grace still holding on to unforgiveness. The power of faith and prayer is linked to your ability to flow in the Spirit, unhindered by offense and unforgiveness. Paul also speaks of the importance of not holding on to complaints (or trespasses) in writing to the Corinthians about love:

> *² If I have the gift of prophecy and I know all the mysteries and everything else, and if I have such complete faith that I can move mountains but I don't have love, I'm nothing… ⁴ Love is patient, love is kind, it isn't jealous, it doesn't brag, it isn't arrogant, ⁵ it isn't rude, it doesn't seek its own advantage, it isn't irritable, it doesn't keep a record of complaints, … ¹³ Now faith, hope, and love remain—these three things—and the greatest of these is love.* (1 Cor 13:2, 4–5, 13 CEB)

Love transforms us; faith and hope sustain us. Let love and grace strengthen your life. Operating in God's love and maintaining a forgiving spirit will empower you to prevail in faith and prayer.

Be Properly Motivated
James warns against wrong motivation in prayer, *"You ask and do not receive, because you ask amiss, that you may spend it on your pleasures."* (James 4:3) God desires to give us good things, but many requests are selfish. When bringing requests to God, His desire is to be glorified, the Gospel shared, and captives freed. When your motive is to *"seek first the kingdom of God and His righteousness"* (Matt. 6:33), then you can trust that God will provide everything you need to complete your assignment.

Does God want to grant you the desires of your heart? Absolutely. When the desires and motives of your heart are pure, unselfish, and align with His character and Word, you can be confident with the petitions you ask of Him.

Ask in Accordance with the Will of God
When we ask for something God has already promised in His Word, we can ask in confidence knowing that we are praying in His will. John writes, *"¹⁴ This is the confidence that we have in our relationship with God: If we ask for anything in agreement with his will, he listens to us. ¹⁵ If we know that he listens to whatever we ask, we know that we have received what we asked from him."* (1 John 5:14–15 CEB)

We can pray according to God's will when we abide in Christ, pray with Jesus' character and nature in mind, and are full of God's faith and perspective. There are times you may need to ask God, "What is Your will in this situation?" Expect God to give understanding as you abide in Him.

Faith that Endures
To prevail in faith and prayer, you need an enduring faith that sees the finish line—the completion of the promise. It is a

faith that gives us hope amidst uncertainty, and sees the promise fulfilled. Enduring faith enables us to run with patience through the challenges of life.

I recently was reminded of the Lord's enduring love for us. Along with our prayer team, Carolyn and I were praying for people after a Sunday service. A middle-aged couple, whom I've never seen before, came up for prayer. As I began to pray, the Holy Spirit gave me an impression. I sensed the Lord say, "They have suffered loss, the loss of a child." Compassion welled within me for them.

I asked the Lord about this word, wanting to be sure before I shared and prayed with them. Again, the impression came, "They have suffered the loss of a child and are grieving." Confident this was the Lord; I shared the word with them: they lost a child and were grieving. She burst into tears and nodded as if to say, "Yes, this is true."

I began to pray for God to heal their broken hearts. The Holy Spirit ministered to them deeply for a few minutes. After receiving ministry, they shared with us they were visiting family in Tucson for a few days and lived in Pennsylvania. They found our church on the internet and felt an impression to come that Sunday.

She then shared with me, "Your word and prayer ministered to us significantly. A year ago, yesterday, I lost my daughter. We felt led yesterday to attend your church today after finding you on the internet. I am so glad we came today!" Carolyn and I comforted them, knowing that the four of us had just experienced a "God moment" that only He could orchestrate. One word—one impression from Jesus—empowers us to continue our race of faith. His word, impression, and visions let us know that He knows, cares and helps us along life's journey.

Let's continue with our discussion of enduring faith. As I shared in a previous chapter, faith is both a fruit of the Spirit and a gift of the Spirit. While we can posture ourselves to develop more faith, ultimately it is God who imparts faith, whether it is a gift of faith or a fruit of the Spirit. There is the gift of faith, but there is also what I like to call the "deposit of faith" that comes from daily relationship with Jesus.

Jesus told the man with the tormented son, *"If you can believe, all things are possible to him who believes."* (Mark 9:23) Jesus is not speaking of intellectual belief or agreement, but a heart-belief that is real faith. Only Jesus can give this type of faith—it is to the heart, not the mind. Belief is an assurance of the mind; faith is an assurance of the heart.

Peter could walk on the water because Jesus said to him, "Come!" Peter believed in his mind that perhaps he could go to Jesus, but once Jesus spoke "come," Peter was assured he could go to Him across the water. As we examined, *"Now faith is the assurance (title deed, confirmation) of things hoped for (divinely guaranteed), and the evidence of things not seen [the conviction of their reality—faith comprehends as fact what cannot be experienced by the physical senses]."* (Heb. 11:1 AMPC)

True faith is an expectant anticipation of the reality of the promise before the manifestation. Faith acts upon God's revealed truth with an assurance of the answer. Peter discovered this truth on the water that night—although briefly!

While faith is assured, nurturing hope is the seedbed from which faith comes. Hope is protection for your mind. Without hope, you will lose stability in your walk with God. Consider your big toes for a moment. They provide "stability" as you walk. Hope could be likened to your big toe! It provides your walk of faith stability.

Faith Works through Love

God's love shed abroad in our hearts creates faith and hope. Paul said that *"now abides these, faith, hope and love."* (1 Cor. 13:13) Hope is a joyful anticipation of the promise. God desires to free us from hopelessness. Love, along with hope, activates our faith. Consider the interaction of love and faith from, *"For [if we are] in Christ Jesus, neither circumcision nor uncircumcision counts for anything, but only faith activated and energized and expressed and working through love."* (Gal. 5:6 AMPC)

Simply stated, faith is expressed through love. Faith is activated, energized, expressed, and works through love. Like epoxy with two components that need to be mixed to be activated, faith needs love to work properly. When faith and love work together something is produced. Faith won't do the job it's created to do unless we ask God to give us love for others. Faith doesn't have power until love is added. Love is the battery. Love does something to faith. Faith communicates what's intended when love is added. Faith works by love.

The Race of Faith

The writer of Hebrews had much to say about enduring faith:

> [1] *Therefore we also, since we are surrounded by so great a cloud of witnesses, let us lay aside every weight, and the sin which so easily ensnares us, and let us run with endurance the race that is set before us,* [2] *looking unto Jesus, the author and finisher of our faith, who for the joy that was set before Him endured*

the cross, despising the shame, and has sat down at the right hand of the throne of God. ³ For consider Him who endured such hostility from sinners against Himself, lest you become weary and discouraged in your souls. ⁴ You have not yet resisted to bloodshed, striving against sin." (Hebrews 12:1–4)

After the in-depth description of faith in Hebrews 11, the writer says, "therefore" and begins chapter 12. Keep in mind that chapters and verses were not added to the Bible until the 13th century. The "therefore" in the beginning of Hebrews 12 is a continuation of the faith discussion in Hebrews 11.

Imagine the exhilaration an Olympic marathon runner experiences as they enter the stadium, packed with cheering spectators, to cross the finish line. Exhausted by the grueling race, the runner can see the finish and knows they are about to cross over.

In my twenties, I ran long-distance races competitively as an amateur, including a couple of half-marathons and many 5K and 10K road races. Every race was challenging. Running competitively taxes your mental and physical endurance. As you near the finish line of a long, tiring race, a cheering crowd gives you a psychological boost to finish your race strong.

For first century Christians reading this epistle, they would have understood the imagery, but perhaps couldn't fully correlate this metaphor to their experience of suffering and persecution. Yet, according to the writer of Hebrews, this is the invisible scenario Christians experience—running a race headed to a triumphant finish line in Christ. As we run our race of faith, we are surrounded by a great cloud of witnesses who have finished before us. They are both Old Testament (OT) and NT heroes of the faith, as well as those through Church history, whose very lives and testimonies cheer us on to run strong and finish well.

The Apostle Paul mentioned frequently the imagery of the Christian life as an athletic race (1 Cor. 9:24–27; Gal. 2:2; Phil. 2:16; 3:14; 1 Tim. 6:12; 2 Tim. 2:5; 4:7; Acts 20:24). To prevail in faith and prayer, and run our race well, we must lay aside every encumbrance that hinders us.

Once while praying, the Lord gave me a vision related to Hebrews 12. I saw Christians trying to run, but they were carrying old, heavy auto parts. It's difficult to run carrying extra weight. Imagine trying to run carrying a heavy car battery? The Lord impressed upon me to remind the Church to "let go of" the heavy and obsolete burdens of the past and run with endurance toward our finish line in Christ.

The Greek verb for the phrase "lay aside," *apotithemai,* can also be translated "to rid oneself" or "throw off."[2] This word is often applied to what people must discard when they become a disciple of Jesus. For example, one would need "to rid oneself" of the works of darkness (Rom. 13:12), the old self (Eph. 4:22), falsehood (Eph. 4:25), anger and gossip (Col. 3:8), moral impurity (Jam. 1:21), and malice and deceit (1 Pet. 2:1).

Like disciplined runners who shed excess body weight and unnecessary clothing, we should remove any extra bulk or burden that would impede our progress to the finish line. Your race—your walk of faith—is not a sprint, but an endurance run that will include some long, uphill climbs and rough terrain. Endurance is one of the essential qualities of the Christian life, *"For you have need of endurance, so that after you have done the will of God, you may receive the promise."* (Heb. 10:36)

I asked the Lord after this vision, "But how Lord? How do believers shed themselves of life's hindrances, run their race well, and finish strong?" Immediately I saw a vision of Jesus smiling and happy on the other side of eternity's finish line. He was waving to me saying, "Come on, you can make it!" A faith that endures is a faith that sees. The answer the Spirit was giving was simple, "Consider the example of Jesus and look upon Him!"

Remember, we should, *"²look unto Jesus, the author and finisher of our faith, who for the joy that was set before Him endured the cross, despising the shame, and has sat down at the right hand of the throne of God. ³ For consider Him who endured such hostility from sinners against Himself, lest you become weary and discouraged in your souls."* (Heb. 12:2–3)

Like Olympic runners who focus their attention on the finish line, we are to focus our attention on Jesus, our older brother who has reached the finish line before us. Consider His example of love, faith, and endurance as you *run*. To run your race well and finish strong, you must look to Jesus, who is the author and finisher of your faith. All true faith begins and ends with Jesus—the Alpha and Omega. When I want more faith, I must seek Him, *I must* look to Him!

Our Endurance of Faith is Anchored in His Endurance

Jesus Himself fixed His eyes on the goal and the joy of bringing humanity across the finish line. Faith works through love, and the byproduct of love and faith is joy—joy inexpressible and full of glory! Hope undergirds faith; it is joyful in anticipation of the promise.

Jesus is the author and perfecter of your faith. You can have God's imparted faith as you learn to keep your focus upon

Christ. Your faith is strengthened as you follow Jesus and understand who you are in Him. He and many others are cheering you on to finish well.

The moment you take your eyes off Jesus, you lose sight of the primary goal of your faith and rob yourself of endurance to run. He is the goal, your destination, and the reason you do what you do. Real faith is rooted in the nature and character of Christ. As you learn to trust Jesus more, His faith will be imparted to you. Prevailing faith that finishes strong begins and ends with Jesus!

Often our sociological and economic conditions dictate our faith level. We need to understand that "with God, nothing is impossible!" No matter who you are, you can make a difference. Your life of faith can impact others, cities, and nations if you know the secret of prevailing faith and prayer.

Chapter Seven

Lord, Teach Us to Pray

"He came back to the disciples and found them sleeping. He said to Peter, "Couldn't you stay alert one hour with me?" Matthew 26:40 CEB

"It is through prayer and intercession that we administer the authority that is ours in the name of Jesus." Derek Prince

Consider that as you give yourself completely to God, confident faith develops. Faith is by His grace, but your participation with God allows the Spirit to strengthen your faith. As you faithfully follow Jesus, your faith grows, and your prayer becomes more confident. Faith and prayer are linked. Faith from God faith leads to confident prayer—nations can be impacted.

Patrick, A Man of Prayer

Beloved by many, fifth century Church leader St. Patrick impacted the nation of Ireland. His perseverance, faith, and courage have encouraged many through the centuries. Did you know that Patrick was not only a bishop in the Church, but he was a devout prayer warrior? The real story of his impact upon Ireland is inspiring.

Patrick was born in Britain around 385 to a Romanized family—his father was a deacon in the Church. When he was sixteen, he was kidnapped by Irish raiders and taken as a slave for six years to Ireland to herd sheep. While in captivity, he learned their language and customs.

At the time, Ireland was a land of Druids and pagans, but Patrick turned to God and prayed frequently. His faith and love for God grew during this time, praying almost continuously. He would write in his memoir, *The Confession*:

> "But after I reached Ireland, I used to pasture the flock each day and I used to pray many times a day. More and more did the love of God, and my fear of him and faith increase, and my spirit was moved so that in a day [I said] from one up to a hundred prayers, and in the night a like number; besides I used to stay out in the forests and on the mountain and I would wake up before daylight to pray in the snow, in icy coldness, in rain, and I used to feel neither ill nor any slothfulness, because, as I now see, the Spirit was burning in me at that time."[1]

Patrick escaped after having a dream from God in which he was told to leave Ireland by going to the coast. There he found some sailors who took him back to Britain. After traveling twenty-eight days through uninhabited country, the men ran out of food.

Here's Patrick's account of what happened next:

> "And after three days we reached land, and for twenty-eight days journeyed through uninhabited country, and the food ran out and hunger overtook them; and one day the steersman began saying: 'Why is it, Christian? You say your God is great and all-powerful; then why can you not pray for us? For we may perish of hunger; it is unlikely indeed that we shall ever see another human being.' In fact, I said to them, confidently: 'Be converted by faith with all your heart to my Lord God, because nothing is impossible for him, so that today he will send food for you on your road, until you be sated, because everywhere he abounds.' And with God's help this came to pass; and behold, a herd of swine appeared on the road before our eyes, and they slew many of them, and remained there for two nights, and the men were full of their meat and well restored, for many of them had fainted and would otherwise have been left half dead by the wayside. And after this they gave the utmost thanks to God, and I was esteemed in their eyes, and from that day they had food abundantly."[2]

Patrick was eventually reunited with his family, who wanted him to stay with them. However, God had other plans. He called Patrick to ministry in Ireland:

"...in a vision of the night, I saw a man whose name was Victoricus coming as if from Ireland with innumerable letters, and he gave me one of them, and I read the beginning of the letter: 'The Voice of the Irish'; and as I was reading the beginning of the letter I seemed at that moment to hear the voice of those who were beside the forest of Foclut which is near the western sea, and they were crying as if with one voice: 'We beg you, holy youth, that you shall come and shall walk again among us.' And I was stung intensely in my heart so that I could read no more, and thus I awoke."[3]

Patrick responded to the call and studied to become a priest, eventually becoming ordained a bishop. He was sent to Ireland in 433 to bring Christianity to the Irish. Patrick worked miracles among the Irish people. Patrick himself wrote that he raised people from the dead, and according to a twelfth century hagiography, there are thirty-three dead raising miracles attributed to Patrick, some of whom are said to have been deceased for many years.[4] These include the raising up of an assortment of women, children, brothers and sisters, princes and princesses. Legend also records Patrick raising a horse from the dead![5]

By far, the biggest miracle was Patrick's ability to teach the Gospel to pagan people and convert them to Christianity. By the end of his life, he had established over three hundred churches and baptized over 120,000 persons in Ireland. He worked in Ireland for over forty years, and died in poverty on March 17, 461. In recognition of his achievements and miracles, Patrick was granted sainthood by the Catholic Church. His death occurred in Saul, the site of the first church he had built in Ireland.[6]

Patrick's devout faith, obedience, and prayer life allowed God to greatly impact Ireland. Patrick wasn't a Christian when he was led as a teenage slave to Ireland, but there he surrendered his life to Christ and became a committed disciple and person of prayer—his life would never be the same. Patrick's prayer life demonstrates that disciples who commit themselves to follow Jesus and learn to pray can expect God's supernatural power to work through them.

Jesus Prayer Life

Jesus set time aside daily to seek the Father's will, direction, and a fresh anointing for his ministry. Here are some examples of Jesus prayer life:

> *[35] Now in the morning, having risen a long while before daylight, He went out and departed to a solitary place; and there He prayed.* (Mark 1:35)

> *So He himself often withdrew into the wilderness and prayed.* (Luke 5:16)

> Jesus *"went out to the mountain to pray and continued all night in prayer"* and chose the twelve. (Luke 6:12)

> *He was alone praying.* (Luke 9:18)

Why did Jesus even need to pray? After all, He was God, right? Yes, Jesus is the eternal Son of God. Jesus, conceived by the

Holy Spirit and born of a woman, is God in human form. As both God and man, Jesus became our example how to live dependent upon Father God and empowered by the Spirit. Daily, He spent time with the Father to know God's will, receive direction, and a fresh anointing for His ministry.

Jesus only did what He saw the Father do. From His prayer life, He lived out of relationship, which allowed God to reveal, direct, and empower Him for ministry. If we are to be like Jesus, we too need to be a people of prayer. I want to look at three of Jesus' priorities that demonstrate His prayer time with the Father were His top priorities.

Jesus Prioritized Prayer over Public Ministry

> *35 Now in the morning, having risen a long while before daylight, He went out and departed to a solitary place; and there He prayed. 36 And Simon and those who were with Him searched for Him. 37 When they found Him, they said to Him, "Everyone is looking for You." 38 But He said to them, "Let us go into the next towns, that I may preach there also, because for this purpose I have come forth." 39 And He was preaching in their synagogues throughout all Galilee, and casting out demons.* (Mark 1:35–39)

Every day was busy for Jesus, well into the evening. Most people know weariness. Every day and week are busy, sometimes a good night's sleep is our highest desire. Jesus prayed in the early morning in a solitary place, *"...having risen a long while before daylight..."* Was He interceding? Yes, but He was primarily spending time with the Father, dialoguing with Him. From that place of fellowship with the Father, Jesus received direction (vs. 38 next towns) and power to preach and minister (vs. 39 preaching and casting out demons).

Petitionary prayer is important; Jesus expects us to bring our needs to Him. But don't make the mistake of reducing prayer to just petition. Prayer is also worship, devotion, and relational dialogue. Make the start of each day a time of fellowship and prayer with God.

In Mark 1:37, notice the pressure of the disciples to help the people, *"Everyone is looking for you."* The pressure of daily life tends to crowd out God. Don't allow the tyranny of the urgent to rob you of your vitality in God! There are always urgent requests and needs, but your time with God daily is one of your top priorities in life.

Daniel's three daily prayers were his top priority, taking time away from his other responsibilities. David prayed morning, noon, and night—no doubt some of these times of prayer were extended times of communion with God. Paul also prayed day and night.

The apostle Paul directed Thessalonian believers to *"pray without ceasing."* (1 Thess. 5:17) I believe we can learn how to commune with God, as normally as we breathe, while still attending to daily affairs. That said, dedicated prayer time with God is also important. Jesus often withdrew to a solitary place to pray. Spending time alone with God is not only important to know Him but also to have influence with Him.

Throughout church history we read of men and women who prioritized prayer with God over public ministry. For example, sixteenth century reformer Martin Luther said, "If I fail to spend two hours in prayer each morning, the Devil gets the victory through the day. I have so much business, I cannot get on without spending three hours daily in prayer."[7]

Early church fathers also placed a high value on prayer, solitude, and meditation with God. They valued moments of silent communication and stillness with God, as much as petitionary prayer and intercession for others. For example, Isaac the Syrian in the seventh century described stillness as, "a deliberate denial of the gift of words for the sake of achieving inner silence, in the midst of which a person can hear the presence of God. It is standing unceasingly, silent, and prayerfully before God."[8]

In my twenties, I worked as an electrical engineer at the Kennedy Space Center in central Florida. It was an hour drive, and I would use my early morning commute to worship and listen to teachings. I also woke up thirty minutes earlier to give myself time for prayer and Bible reading before I left for the day. Quiet time with God is different than commute time with God! It's still something I value today and would recommend to everyone, even if your schedule is busy and you have a long commute to work.

I place a high value on waiting before the Lord early each morning. I've discovered that solitude and quiet reflection enable me to commune with Him and hear what is on His heart. This positions me for more specific moments of prayer and Bible reflection during my quiet time with Him.

Many Christians want the answer without the discipline. Prayer is an intentional time of communion with God. Through prayer, we enter an understanding of the heart and will of God. Our prayer becomes empowered through our communion with God and knowing His word. Prayer is vitally important if we are going to live a victorious Christian life.

Jesus Prayed in Moments of Decision

> *[12] Now it came to pass in those days that He went out to the mountain to pray and continued all night in prayer to God. [13] And when it was day, He called His disciples to Himself; and from them He chose twelve whom He also named apostles...* (Luke 6:12–13)

In this passage, Jesus went out to the mountain to pray. Mountains in Scripture are frequently a location for time with God. The conversation perhaps went something like this, "Father, what is your direction, which of these should I choose?" We all face major decisions and crossroads in life. Learn to value quality time with God in prayer to hear from Him, get His perspective and direction.

By the way, sometimes the direction God gives is wisdom and peace. Proverbs tells us: *"Happy is the man who finds wisdom, and the man who gains understanding; ... Her ways are ways of pleasantness, and all her paths are peace."* (Prov. 3:13, 17) Wisdom or understanding leads to peace. Hearing, or receiving God's peace, is at times the greatest prophetic word you will ever receive. Learn to value His presence and peace as much as a directive word from Him.

Prior to moving to Arizona in 2001, we earnestly sought God's will and direction. Yet, He gave us no clear word or direction. Instead, God provided wise counsel through my father-in-law and others, and He gave us peace about the decision. It seemed like the right decision and direction for us, and God's wisdom and peace comforted and guided us.

After I accepted the job offer in Tucson, the next morning God gave me a "clear word," confirming this was His will and direction for us. In fact, He said, "You will excel in your job, your family will flourish, and your ministry will prosper. Can I not make streams in the desert?" But in this case, before He gave a clear word and direction, He used wisdom and peace to guide us. Prayer allowed us to enter a place with God where He could guide with His eye (Psalm 32:8). His peace confirmed the path we were to take before He gave a confirming word to us. God was bringing us into a greater place of faith and trust in Him.

Jesus Prayed to Stay Focused on His Assignment

> *[22] Immediately Jesus made His disciples get into the boat and go before Him to the other side, while He sent the multitudes away. [23] And when He had sent the multitudes away, He went up on the mountain by Himself to pray. Now when evening came, He was alone there.* (Matt. 14:22–23)

Jesus multiplied the loaves and fishes for the multitude, and then sent the disciples in a boat to the other side of the lake before Him. He sent the crowd away and went to the top of the mountain to pray. He was there alone, in prayer, focusing on His purpose. Why?

John's account of the same miracle in chapter six of his gospel gives us the answer: the people wanted to make Jesus king after they saw He was the "bread maker." But Jesus knew that there were unreached people groups He needed to impact. To do so, they needed to get to the other side of the lake to Gennesaret (Matt. 14:34–36). Jesus stayed focused on His purpose and assignments through prayer.

Do you have a place to get alone with God, to stay focused on your assignment? Every believer has a purpose, beginning with following Christ. Beyond that, He empowers us to represent Him to the world. Prayer positions you to hear God and refocus on His will for your life. Prayer renews vision through ongoing encounters with the Lord.

The Lord's Prayer Model

Because prayer was central to the ministry of Jesus, He wanted it to be foundational in the lives of his disciples. When the disciples asked Jesus to teach them to pray, He responded by giving them a prayer model—often referred to as the Lord's Prayer. However, what we call the Lord's Prayer could be labeled "the Disciple's Prayer," as it's an outline or guide for prayer. Like the early disciples, we also want to know effective principles of prayer and kingdom ministry.

> *[1] Now it came to pass, as He was praying in a certain place, when He ceased, that one of His disciples said to Him, "Lord, teach us to pray, as John also taught his disciples." [2] So, He said to them, "When you pray, say: Our Father in heaven, Hallowed be Your name. Your kingdom come. Your will be done on earth as it is in heaven. [3] Give us day by day our daily bread. [4] And forgive us our sins, for we also forgive everyone who is indebted to us. And do not lead us into temptation but deliver us from the evil one. (Luke 11:1–4)*

Luke's gospel primarily encourages the reader to persist in prayer. Matthew's gospel also gives an account of the Lord's Prayer. However, Luke's context of "Our Father" is different from that of Matthew, which is situated among critiques of three acts of religion (Matt. 6:1–8). The latter's audience are "Jewish opponents of Mathew's community," who are accustomed to the practice of prayer. Thus, Matthew is correcting their improper practices of prayer (Matt. 6:5–14).

In Matthew's account, Jesus focuses on the motivation for prayer. He is teaching disciples to be careful not to practice prayer before people, to be admired. Rather, they should seek the Father's admiration. In contrast, Luke's context is within a Gentile community, most of whom are not accustomed to prayer. Luke instructs the Gentiles about how to pray, emphasizing a positive (persistent) attitude in prayer.

Let's examine some of the components of this model of prayer taught by Jesus.

Praying in a Certain Place

Jesus arrived at Bethany, a favorite location and home to Mary, Martha, and Lazarus. Jesus felt at home and relaxed here. For example, He spent the night in Bethany before His triumphal entry into Jerusalem.

We all have places like this. We often refer to them as "prayer closets." It's important to establish a place, or places, where it is conducive to establishing a consistent prayer life. It may be a room in your home, outside on the porch, or taking a walk.

My prayer closet is my home office. We've lived in this house for eighteen years, and my office has become my prayer closet. God's presence lingers in my office, and I cherish my time with God in this place. In some ways, it has become my Bethel (Gen 28). In fact, the direction to plant Passion Church in Tucson began with my time with God in my home office—it is a sacred place for me.

If you don't have a place like this, the first step to a powerful prayer life is to discover your "prayer closet" and frequent it daily with God. I also love to take long walks and pray, which is a precious time and highly effective. But it's my home office that is the place of deep communion and revelation of prayer that I value the most.

However, realize that God is always present with you. Learning to abide in God's presence continually leads to a consistent prayer life—even when you are not in your favorite place to pray. Prayer is simply communion with God. As we follow Jesus daily, communion and conversation with Him should be as normal as breathing as we go about each day's affairs.

Lord, Teach Us to Pray

The disciples had witnessed Jesus' supernatural lifestyle. But, why did they ask, "Teach us to pray," and not "Teach us to heal or deliver oppressed?" The disciples watched Jesus heal the sick. They witnessed His miraculous power to open the eyes of the blind and ears of the deaf. They observed Him cleanse a leper with the touch of His hand. His words calmed a stormy sea and raised the dead to life. How did Jesus do these healings and miracles?

What was the secret to Jesus' miracle power? It was mysterious to them at first, but eventually the disciples learned His secret. Jesus had this power because He was a man of prayer! The disciples watched Jesus pray and realized His prayer life was a component to His power. Jesus desired that every disciple would learn how to pray and operate in His greater works (John 14:12).

Fully God and fully man, Jesus' life gives us an example of how to live dependent upon God for victorious living. It begins with being a person of prayer and a student of God's Word. At the very beginning of Jesus' earthly ministry, we read how Jesus was led by the Spirit into the wilderness to pray and fast for forty days, *"Then Jesus, being filled with the Holy Spirit, returned from the Jordan and was led by the Spirit into the wilderness..."* (Luke 4:1).

Next, we read of Satan tempting Jesus in the wilderness. Jesus overcomes the devil's schemes by quoting God's Word in truth. Luke records, *"Jesus returned in the power of the Spirit to Galilee, and news of Him went out through all the surrounding region."* (Luke 4:14)

Jesus obeyed the leading of the Spirit into the wilderness. His discipline of prayer prepared Him for the empowerment of the Spirit after He left the wilderness. As I shared earlier in this chapter, Jesus was God on earth, but in His humanity, He lived dependent upon the Father and the Holy Spirit (John 5:19). Therefore, He became an example to His followers how to live dependent upon God's leading and empowerment.

To mature in faith and prayer, like Jesus, we need to be consistently led and empowered by the Spirit. This requires intentional discipline. However, we often want the empowerment without the discipline. Prayer can be relaxed, free-flowing, and intimate. But prayer is also times of disciplined communion with God. Through prayer, we enter a deeper understanding of the heart and will of God. Our prayer becomes empowered through our intimacy with God.

There are no short cuts to spiritual vitality—it's about abiding in Christ and God's Word daily. Prayer should not be done out of duty but from a place of love and desire to be with Jesus, the author and perfecter of our faith.

Praise and Worship

Prayer should begin with praise and worship, *"Our Father in heaven, hallowed be your name..."* To hallow means to sanctify, to set apart, to make special.

As a Christian, when we call God "Father," we are acknowledging God as the loving, eternal Father of creation, who is all-powerful, all-knowing, and ever-present. In so doing, we set Him apart as Holy and special—we hallow Him. But not everyone can call God "Father," only those who, through Jesus, have entered a relationship with God and become members of His family. *"But as many as received Him, to them He gave the right to become children of God, to those who believe in His name."* (John 1:12)

Our existence and life in Christ are a result of the love and goodness of Father God. *"Every good gift, every perfect gift, comes from above. These gifts come down from the Father..."* (James 1:17 CEB). Our response back to God is worship, which is the first element of prayer. Some disciples miss this element of prayer. Perhaps due to a lack of relationship with God, prayer for some Christians is just a means to receive help in emergencies. God wants to help in our time of need, but it's not the only purpose of prayer.

God desires relationship with us. When we worship Him in Spirit and truth, we will discover the resurrection power of Christ working in us (John 4:23). Relationship yields worship. Praise, worship, and thanksgiving bring us into the presence of God (Psalm 100:4–5). This is where genuine prayer originates.

Hearts that worship are hearts that realize the power of faith and prayer!

Prayer Should Have Expectation

We are to pray, *"your kingdom come, your will be done."* In the NT, the Kingdom of God or Kingdom of Heaven is mentioned approximately eighty times. The English word *kingdom* is from the Greek word *basileia,* which primarily means: 1) the authority to rule as a king, 2) the realm over which the reign is exercised.[9]

Asking for God's kingdom to come is not a "millennial" prayer focus. It's not a request for the second coming of Christ to liberate us from this world. Rather, it is inviting our Father and benevolent King to rule, and for the realm of His Kingdom to reign presently. We eagerly wait for the promise of Jesus' coming, but as we wait, we endeavor to disciple nations in His name.

We are to change our thinking (repent), believe the gospel, and submit to the reign of God's kingdom. *"[14] Now after John was put in prison, Jesus came to Galilee, preaching the gospel of the kingdom of God, [15] and saying, "The time is fulfilled, and the kingdom of God is at hand. Repent, and believe in the gospel."* (Mark 1:14–15)

Asking for God's kingdom to come is to ask for the King to rule over His realm—which in simplest terms is Lordship over our lives and world. It begins with us inviting His rule over our lives and allowing His throne to be established in our hearts. We must recognize the importance of submitting our will to His will. Hearts unsubmitted to God's Lordship may pray amiss.

Have you ever prayed a "misdirected prayer?" Most of us have. My definition of a "misdirected prayer" is a prayer that is motivated by our desire and will, rather than led by the Holy Spirit and God's will.

I'm grateful Jesus didn't answer all my prayers when I was a new Christian. Perhaps you can relate. As I've matured in Christ, I realize that not all my prayers were from the heart of God. Learning how to pray and commune with God as a loving relationship is a key principle to an effective prayer life. A heart filled with hurt, offense, unforgiveness, and judgment often prays in a misguided way.

Do you remember the story of James and John wanting to call down fire upon a Samaritan village because they rejected Jesus? Look at the response of Jesus to their misdirected request:

> *⁵⁴ And when His disciples James and John saw this, they said, "Lord, do You want us to command fire to come down from heaven and consume them, just as Elijah did?" ⁵⁵ But He turned and rebuked them, and said, "You do not know what manner of spirit you are of. ⁵⁶ For the Son of Man did not come to destroy men's lives but to save them." And they went to another village.* (Luke 9:54–56)

Have you ever wanted someone to receive "justice?" Have you desired for someone to get what they deserve? The Samaritan village rejected Jesus, and in the minds of James and John, they deserved God's judgment. But Jesus makes it clear that God's way is love and forgiveness—mercy triumphs over judgment and vengeance belongs to God alone.

We are in the New Covenant age of grace where God's love through Jesus is given to humanity. God is not willing for any to perish, but for all to turn to Him, as God is reconciling the world to Himself through Christ. Calling fire down, or desiring judgment on others, isn't God's will or way. God's love, demonstrated through the power of the cross and resurrection of Jesus, is greater than humanity's sin, bad behavior, and brokenness.

If my prayer is an attempt to get God to do my will, it is misdirected. Prayer should be motivated by a desire to realize God's will for our lives, families, relationships, workplaces, churches, etc. Conversely, when we pray according to God's heart and will, we are confident that He has heard us and, in His time, and way our prayer will be answered. It begins with a love for Jesus and desire to be with Him. That's the essence of all prayer—communion with God and a love for His presence.

Since God's kingdom is near, we should expect God's kingdom to reign supreme over our lives and remain hopeful that prayers and promises will be answered. This type of faith develops through committed discipleship and extended times of prayer. Half-hearted prayer will not build expectation for breakthrough!

Prayer Should Have Petition
"Give us day by day our daily bread." Petitioning God is basic to prayer and Jesus taught us to pray for our daily needs. The first three requests in the Lord's prayer deal with God's glory, "Your name, "Your Kingdom, "Your will." The last three requests have to do with us, "Give us," forgive us," and "lead us."

When Jesus said, *"Give us today our daily bread,"* He was making the point that it is okay to pray for our daily needs. We are to seek God first and His kingdom, and then be confident in the asking. We can't serve God and do His will without food, clothing, and other essential needs. God knows our needs, cares for us, and promises to provide!

God is a good Father who enjoys giving to His children. A child has rights in a family. He desires to give all good things to us if we just ask Him according to His character, nature, and word. Jesus confirms this truth: *"How much more will your Father who is in Heaven give good things to those who ask Him."* (Matt. 7:11)

In John's gospel, Jesus instructs us to ask the Father in His name: *"²³ At that time you won't need to ask me for anything. I tell you the truth, you will ask the Father directly, and he will grant your request because you use my name. ²⁴ You haven't done this before. Ask, using my name, and you will receive, and you will have abundant joy."* (John 16:23–24 NLT)

In John 16:27, Jesus explains why this works—we believe in Him, *"for the Father Himself loves you, because you have loved Me, and have believed that I came forth from God."* Therefore, we are partakers of the inheritance of the only begotten Son of God. As Paul writes in Romans, we are *"heirs of God and joint-heirs with Christ."* (Rom. 8:17) The more time spent with God in prayer, the more confident you will be in asking! God grants requests to those with persistent faith.

Confession Should be an Integral Part of Prayer

"Forgive us our sins." In Christ, you have been forgiven and your sins have been cast into a sea of forgetfulness. But Jesus' prayer model keeps us humble before God and reliant upon His grace. Healthy introspection is needed daily. *"If we confess*

our sins, He is faithful and just to forgive us our sins and to cleanse us from all unrighteousness." (John 1:9)

There are times when sharing our sins with others is appropriate. James writes that there is healing virtue with this type of prayer: *"Confess your sins to each other and pray for each other so that you may be healed. The earnest prayer of a righteous person has great power and produces wonderful results."* (James 5:16 NLT)

However, I would also caution against becoming too introspective. While confession is necessary, don't live there. If you dwell on your mistakes to long, you will give in to the voice of condemnation and criticalness. If you err, confess your faults to God, and if needed, confess to a mature believer(s) who can pray with you as James instructs. Then believe and receive God's love and forgiveness and move on—don't stay camped in your mistakes and failures. Your identity is not defined by your faults, but in Christ.

Forgiveness is Vital to Effective Prayer

"Forgive everyone who..." In the Lord's model for prayer, Jesus instructs us to ask for our daily needs, but there is a condition. Connected to asking for daily needs is His requirement to forgive others. Jesus links the two petitions so we would recognize our need for forgiveness as well. He expects us to extend the grace of forgiveness to others.

St. Augustine labeled this request, "the terrible petition" because if we pray, "Forgive us our sins, for we also forgive everyone who is indebted to us..." and at the same time harbor unforgiveness, we are asking God not to forgive us.[10]

When John Wesley served as a missionary to the American Colonies, it is said that he had a difficult time with General James

Oglethorpe, who was known for his pride and harshness. On one occasion, Oglethorpe declared, "I never forgive." Wesley replied, "Then sir, I hope you never sin!"[11] To sin is human; therefore, to forgive others is the essence of grace received.

A condition of effective prayer is maintaining a forgiving spirit, *"25And whenever you stand praying, if you have anything against anyone, forgive him, that your Father in heaven may also forgive you your trespasses. 26 But if you do not forgive, neither will your Father in heaven forgive your trespasses."* (Mark 11:25–26)

I've never met anyone who didn't want their daily needs met, but I have met many who won't forgive others. Extending forgiveness to others is foundational to our life in Christ, having prayer answered, and having our needs met. The enemy knows this and attempts to ensnare us in unforgiveness and offense. Later in the Lord's prayer, we are to ask God to empower us to overcome temptation. Perhaps one of the most common temptations many experience is offense toward others. Left unchecked, it leads to unforgiveness, which inhibits your spiritual vitality and hinders prayers from being answered.

The power of faith and prayer is linked to your ability to live unhindered from offense and unforgiveness. You can't walk in the fullness of grace holding on to unforgiveness.

Trusting in God's Protective Ability

"Do not lead us into temptation but deliver us from the evil one." Some scholars suggest that Jesus is using a figure of speech called a *litotes* (pronounced ˈlī-tə-tēz), which expresses something positive by negating its opposite.[12] For example, we might say, "This desert isn't bad is it?" Meaning, "this desert is pretty good!"

When we pray, "Do not lead us into temptation..." what we are really saying is, "Keep me away from temptation..." We pray, "God, don't let the enemy ensnare me in a trap!" "God help me not give into temptation and the schemes of the evil one."

To be tempted is human. Jesus, who never sinned was tempted but didn't succumb to temptation. Paul states that God provides a way to escape temptation, *"No temptation has seized you that isn't common for people. But God is faithful. He won't allow you to be tempted beyond your abilities. Instead, with the temptation, God will also supply a way out so that you will be able to endure it."* (1 Cor. 10:13 CEB)

As we mature in Christ, we are empowered to overcome temptation. We're not beyond sin, but the Holy Spirit is affecting the victory of Christ within us. This is the power of Jesus' grace at work in our lives by the Spirit and God's Word. We should have more confidence in God's ability to protect and keep us than in the enemy's ability to tempt, attack, or destroy us. In fact, God gives His angels charge over you to keep you in all your ways!

God promises to deliver you in every circumstance. Trust him! *"Call upon Me in the day of trouble; I will deliver you, and you shall glorify Me."* (Psalm 50:15)

The Doxology

In Luke's account of the Lord's prayer, the doxology is missing. Look at Matthew's account, *"...For Yours is the kingdom and the power and the glory forever. Amen."* (Matt. 6:13)

Early Greek manuscripts of the NT omitted the doxology in both gospel accounts. Later, in the second and third century manuscripts of the NT, we see the doxology added to

Matthew's gospel. Many scholars believe this is due to the early church wanting to end on a triumphant note, rather than simply asking to be freed from temptation. While this doxology may not have been given directly by Jesus, we see echoes of this in both the OT and NT.

Yours, O LORD, is the greatness, the power and the glory, the victory and the majesty; ... Yours is the kingdom... (1 Chr. 29:11)

...Blessing and honor and glory and power Be to Him who sits on the throne, and to the Lamb, forever and ever! (Rev. 5:13)

Chapter Eight

Do You Have the Right to Ask?

"If you abide in Me, and My words abide in you, you will ask what you desire, and it shall be done for you." John 15:7

"If you want anything from God, you will have to pray into heaven. That is where it all is. If you live in the earth realm and expect to receive from God, you will never get anything." Smith Wigglesworth

There are different aspects to prayer. At a foundational level, prayer should be delightful communion with our creator, savior, and friend. But prayer is also petitionary. As I shared in the previous chapter, Jesus directs us to *"ask for our daily bread."* God expects us to ask for our needs, even though He already knows our need. Prayer is also intercession on behalf of others.

When it comes to petitionary or intercessory prayer, "Do you have the right to ask God for your requests?" The answer might surprise you. Let's use the parable of the vine Jesus gave in John 15 to answer this question.

Jesus, the one true Vine

> *¹I am the true vine, and My Father is the vinedresser. ² Every branch in Me that does not bear fruit He takes away; and every branch that bears fruit He prunes, that it may bear more fruit. ³ You are already clean because of the word which I have spoken to you. ⁴ Abide in Me, and I in you. As the branch cannot bear fruit of itself, unless it abides in the vine, neither can you, unless you abide in Me. ⁵ "I am the vine, you are the branches. He who abides in Me, and I in him, bears much fruit; for without Me you can do nothing. ⁶ If anyone does not abide in Me, he is cast out as a branch and is withered; and they gather them and throw them into the fire, and they are burned. ⁷ If you abide in Me, and My words abide in you, you will ask what you desire, and it shall be done for you. ⁸ By this My Father is glorified, that you bear much fruit; so you will be My disciples.* (John 15:1–8)

Within Jewish tradition, the vine was a symbol for Israel. God brought a vine out of Egypt and planted it in the Promised Land (Psalm 80:8–18). It had been ravaged by wild animals and needed protection and reestablishment. The prophet Isaiah reveals that the vineyard of Israel has borne wild grapes instead of proper ones (Isaiah 5). Other OT prophets used the same picture to illustrate Israel as a vine that has been ravaged.

In John's gospel, Jesus is declaring that He is the "true vine" or the "true Israel." He is the one on whom God's purposes are now resting. His followers are members of God's true people, if they remain in Him. This parable is about Jesus and His people. Jesus concludes the parable about fruitfulness, *"By this my Father is glorified, that you bear much fruit, so you will be my disciples."* (John 15:8)

Jesus openly declares the Father desires the followers of Jesus to bear fruit. This fruitfulness should be two-fold. First, it is the development of Godly character in one's life, or as Paul describes in Galatians 5, fruit of the Spirit. Secondly, Christians should be bearing fruit in the kingdom of God, i.e. reaching the lost, setting people free, healing the sick, and making disciples—resulting in the expansion of God's Kingdom.

A few verses later, Jesus makes this bold statement to his disciples, *"You did not choose Me, but I chose you and appointed you that you should go and bear fruit, and that your fruit should remain, that whatever you ask the Father in My name He may give you."* (John 15:16) He reinforces the concept that His disciples should be fruitful. But He also gives three important principles as to how we can be fruitful in our Christian life.

Know you are Chosen by God
First, it is vital that you and I understand that our acceptance of Jesus brings us into sonship with God and adoption into God's family. This gives us security and confidence as we carry out the Father's work. Our sonship is foundational to praying with conviction and assurance that God hears and answers prayer.

Know you are Appointed by God
Second, each of us has been appointed to bear fruit and given an assignment, purpose, and destiny by God that only we can fulfill. To aid us in being fruitful in our assignment, God has promised to meet our every need in this pursuit.

Know you are Promised by God.
Third, in this parable, we have a clear promise by Jesus that God will answer prayer as we endeavor to bear kingdom fruit. We need to have a firm conviction of the faithfulness of God to answer prayer; He wants us to not only be fruitful but for our fruit to endure! Let's unpack the parable to understand these truths.

Ask What You Desire
"If you abide in Me, and My words abide in you, you will ask what you desire, and it shall be done for you." (John 15:7) Do you notice how clearly Jesus states that we should expect answers to our prayer? But there are conditions. Before I go further with this verse and parable, let me ask you some questions.

Do you have the right to demand anything from God? How bold do you dare to be in prayer? What are your rights, your limitations, and your boundaries when it comes to the issue of prayer? I'm asking these questions because I find that many people struggle with being direct and bold in prayer. Yet, I believe Jesus is inviting us, through this parable and other teachings, to be confident and direct with God when praying.

The above questions are answered by two other questions: Are you abiding in Christ, and does His word abide in you? John 15:4 says, *"Abide in Me, and I in you. As the branch cannot bear fruit of itself, unless it abides in the vine, neither can you, unless you abide in Me."* In other words, our boldness and confidence in prayer is connected to our intimacy with Jesus—through prayer (communion with Him) and His Word.

The English word *abide* in John 15:4 is translated from the Greek word *ménō*. *Ménō* means primarily to stay in relation, to continue, to remain, to abide, and to endure—a. "to stay in a place," figuratively "to remain in a sphere," b. "to stand against opposition," "to hold out," "to stand fast," c. "to stay still," and d. "to remain," "to endure," "to stay in force."[1] *Ménō* implies that there is action required on our part. We are to abide, remain, endure, or stand fast in the Lord.

We've been united with Christ through faith and work of the Spirit, but we must also choose to remain in Christ, allowing His Word to fill us. In other words, we must be intentional about our relationship with Him.

Oswald Chambers, an early twentieth century Christian evangelist, teacher, and author of the devotional *My Utmost for His Highest*, said this regarding abiding in Christ, "The disciple who abides in Jesus *is* the will of God, and his apparently free choices are God's foreordained decrees. Mysterious? Logically contradictory and absurd? Yes, but a glorious truth to a saint."[2] Your abiding in Christ is the very will of God, and your "random" choices are part of God's intended purpose for your life. This is mysterious indeed!

Your prayer life will also grow through your deepening relationship with Jesus. All fruitfulness is linked to your intimacy with Christ. Out of intimate relationship with God, you're asking strengthens to confident assurance. Remaining in Him and His Word builds faith and trust that He will answer your prayers and meet your needs. Your understanding of God changes as your mind is renewed. Prayer now flows from intimacy with Jesus, and expectation for answers is the outflow of one's abiding relationship.

Rolland Baker said this about prayer and intimacy with God,

> "The Christian life is first and foremost a romance with God—we should feel God's love. Prayer isn't hard work, a struggle between our will and God's. Prayer is communion with God and should be the freest and most intimate of all communication. Miracles, church growth, revival, and transformation are all excellent, but nothing compares to simply being in love with Jesus. Love is the outflow of our intimacy with Christ."

When your focus is on Jesus and abiding in Him, love flows, and promises are realized. All fruitfulness in life is discovered through abiding in Jesus and God's Word—the one true vine.

The Importance of Asking

Jesus used an attention-grabbing word in John 15:7, when He was speaking to the disciples about prayer. *Ask* in this verse is from the Greek word *aitéo* and silences the religious suggestion that we are unworthy with no rights to come into the presence of God. It also refutes the concept that we must pitifully beg the Lord for the things we have need. *Aitéo* means to be adamant in requesting and demanding assistance to meet tangible needs, such as food, shelter, money, and so forth. *Aitéo* also means to ask with urgency, even to the point of demanding—"to ask for, to demand, to beg of, to demand of."[3]

Although this word *aitéo* means to demand or insist, it does not give a believer the right to be arrogant or rude in his or her approach to God. In the NT, the word *aitéo* is used to portray a person addressing a superior. The person may insist or demand that certain needs be met, but he approaches and speaks to his superior with respect and honor.

The word *aitéo* also expresses the idea that one possesses a full expectation to receive what was firmly requested. The word *aitéo* used in John 15:7 primarily has to do with requesting things of a physical and material nature—such as food, clothes, shelter, money, and so on. Jesus said plainly that we are to pursue God's kingdom and righteousness foremost, and He promises to provide for our material needs (Matt. 6:33).

Jesus said in Luke's gospel, *"Do not fear, little flock, for it is your Father's good pleasure to give you the kingdom."* (Luke 12:32) God desires to freely give us the benefits of His kingdom. Keep in mind that God's kingdom is the right of our king to rule, and the domain over which God rules. When we pray, *"Your kingdom come"* from the Lord's prayer model, we are asking for God's rule and domain to take precedent over our lives.

Additionally, God the Father, as a just and benevolent king, desires to provide abundantly for the citizens of His kingdom. Even in medieval times, good kings desired to take care of their kingdoms. How much more will the High King of Heaven who is just and righteous? Our heavenly Father and King promises to take care of us! Yet, He is expecting us to ask, through petitionary prayer with confidence. We are to "make a demand" upon heaven, as we confidently abide in Jesus, expecting our prayers to be answered and fruit to result. Truly, the Father is glorified when we are fruitful in every aspect of our lives.

In Luke's gospel, Jesus instructs the disciples how to pray, petition, and persist in prayer, *"⁹ So I say to you, ask, and it will be given to you; seek, and you will find; knock, and it will be opened to you. ¹⁰ For everyone who asks receives, and he who seeks finds, and to him who knocks it will be opened."* (Luke 11:9–10) The English word *ask*, in the phrase *"ask, and it will be given to you,"* also translates from the Greek word *aitéo* in the Greek present tense—implying continual asking. Jesus instructs us to ask, and to continue to ask, believing that the answer will manifest. How long do you pray? Keep praying until you receive the answer, or the Spirit gives you assurance the prayer is answered.

When you know you are praying according to the will of God, you don't have to sheepishly utter your requests. You can boldly assert your faith and expect God to move on your behalf. God invites you to pray confidently and courageously, and to continue to pray until the answer is realized. Act upon His revealed will and make a demand of heaven until the promise manifests. You must ask and continue to ask until you see the object of your prayer.

Some are bothered by this idea of "demanding" something from God. However, we shouldn't find this concept of prayer disturbing if we keep the words of Jesus in context. First and foremost, God is our loving Father. He delights in meeting our needs and giving good gifts to His children. Once again, the first part of John 15:7 gives us the key, *"If you abide (or remain) in Me, and My words abide (or remain) in you ... "* Relationship breeds confidence in God's promises. Meditating on God's Word builds faith and assurance of God's willingness to answer prayer and back up His promises.

To underscore this point, look at what Jesus said in Matthew's gospel, *"How much more will your Father who is in Heaven give good things to those who ask Him."* (Matt 7:11) You have a right, as His daughter or son, to come boldly before God and ask Him for the things you need and for the desires of your heart. In fact, He expects you to do so! Remain in Him and be confident in your relationship and His promises.

Conversely, James teaches that believers often fail to see prayer answered because they simply don't ask (*aitéo*), or they ask with a wrong motive. *"You long for something you don't have, so you commit murder. You are jealous for something you can't get, so you struggle and fight. You don't have because you don't ask."* (James 4:2 CEB) James was confronting disciples who were ruled by their carnal nature. Some were controlled by jealousy, fighting and striving with others to obtain what they desired. James response to their wrong attitudes and behavior, *"You don't have because you don't ask (aitéo)."*

When we abide in Christ confidently, we cease from striving and learn to ask with joy for the things we need and desire. Carnal Christians operate from fear, jealousy, envy, and strife, attempting to obtain what others have through wrong means and motives. A sign of mature faith is confidently abiding in Jesus and His Word, asking of the Father what one needs and desires assertively and with humility.

Asking for Help in Haiti

Prior to moving to Haiti as missionaries, the Lord told Carolyn that He would bring someone to help us with our infant daughter Hannah. This didn't make sense at first, as we didn't think we needed help in the home or with our daughter. However,

God's word empowered us to pray with confidence and expectation for the help we would need.

After being in Haiti just a few weeks, it was apparent we needed help. Daily life in Haiti was difficult compared to life in the States. The lack of electricity, running water (we had cistern on the roof that collected rainwater for cleaning and bathing, but not potable), and a lack of appliances were a few of our new challenges. Our home had no washer or dryer. Laundry was washed by hand and hung out daily to dry. Most of our meals were shopped for and prepared daily. Additionally, most Haitians need work, and it is expected that you will hire help for the house and yard. Despite having little money as missionaries, we needed the assistance and they needed work.

We had moved into an adorable little home on a mountain top overlooking Port-au-Prince. We rented the house from other missionaries who were out of the country on sabbatical. A Haitian maid, Elizabeth, had worked for them, and we initially kept her employed with for us.

Unfortunately, a few weeks later we discovered that Elizabeth was routinely stealing food and some jewelry had come up missing. When Carolyn discovered this, we realized that Elizabeth wasn't the one the Lord had promised. God said this person would be a blessing to our family, someone Carolyn could bond with and entrust with our infant daughter. We began to pray in earnest for the person God intended to come into our home. Carolyn frequently heard, "not yet" from Him. She had God's peace and knew this person would be with us soon.

One Sunday morning while Carolyn was praying, the Lord spoke to her, "I am bringing the promised helper to you at church this morning, and she will approach you about a job." We arrived at church early and spent time in prayer with the other missionaries and Haitian leaders before the service. Immediately after prayer, the director of the ministry came to us and said there was a Haitian woman who had just arrived at the church, and when she saw us, she told the director that "God sent her to us, and she was to work for us."

This woman, Denise, told the ministry director God sent her to work for a young missionary couple with a young baby that just arrived in Haiti, and to come to our church that morning to meet us, even though it wasn't her home church. The director was understandably cautious with the assertiveness of this young woman, since she knew nothing about her or God's word to Carolyn about a helper for us.

Carolyn, recalling God's promise to her that our helper would be sent to us at church that morning, immediately said, "Yes, I want to meet her." Upon meeting Denise, Carolyn immediately connected with her and felt a love for her. Our infant daughter, Hannah, reached for Denise—she had never done this before. We hired Denise that morning, and she started working for us that week!

Denise worked with us for a year while we were in Haiti. She was a tremendous blessing to our family. She was full of the Lord' joy, loved us, and we loved her. She brought Hannah flowers from the roadside many mornings. She was a vibrant Christian from a good Christian family, who would sing and pray as she worked. Denise and our family shared stories of God's goodness, presence, healings, and miraculous provision.

As we were packing to leave Haiti, a missionary friend, Marilyn, came to help us. Marilyn was fluent in Creole, and

Denise asked her to interpret a message for us. It was only then that we discovered the intricate details of each other's stories, and how God divinely brought us together.

Denise shared that she had been working for another missionary woman who had to return to the United States because of a medical condition and lost her job. She prayed and asked God to send her to her next employer. One evening God gave her a dream; she saw a young American couple with a small baby. Prior to meeting us, Denise was interviewed for another job with another family, but didn't take it because they were not the people she saw in the dream.

Denise's mother was worried about her family's finances, since Denise's previous job helped them considerably. In Haiti, jobs are scarce, and the pay is little. Haitians need constant work just to survive. Most families—parents, siblings, grandparents, and grandchildren—usually live together in small one to two room homes, sharing a community well and toilet with other neighbors. Everyone works hard as a family unit to provide for each other. A community's survival depends on working closely together.

Understandably, Denise's mother wanted her to take any job that she was offered, but Denise told her she had to obey what the Lord revealed in her dream and wait. We're not sure how long Denise went without a job, but the Sunday morning she met us, the Lord said to her that she would meet us that day. That same morning, her mother was also praying, and the Lord revealed the church where Denise was to meet us. Denise obeyed the revelation given by her mother and met us that Sunday at our church!

When we heard Denise's account of God bringing us together, we were astounded! We observed, once again, the power of prevailing faith and prayer. Faith is the joyful anticipation of the promise!

Prayer, Thanksgiving, and Rejoicing Releases Heaven's Peace and Joy

Paul wrote to the Philippian believers to *"Be anxious for nothing; but in everything by prayer and supplication with thanksgiving, let your requests be made known to God."* (Phil. 4:6) The English word *request* is translated from a Greek word *aít ma*, which has at its root the Greek word *aitéo*. By using *aitéo* in this verse, Paul urges us to be bold, authoritative and commanding in our prayers. However, Paul underscores the point that our approach to God must not be rude and arrogant but rather filled with gratefulness and thanksgiving.

The word *aitéo* implies that one possesses an expectation to receive what was firmly requested. God promises to abundantly provide for us (John 10:10). It is also the Father's good pleasure, as our benevolent King, to provide for us from His kingdom. We are instructed to not fear but to pray and trust Him (Luke 12:32).

Peace is to be a normal characteristic of Christians. Unfortunately, many believers find themselves filled with worry and fear instead of peace. Paul give us important insights to receive answers to prayer and live worry free in his letter to the Philippians:

> *⁴ Always be full of joy in the Lord. I say it again—rejoice! ...*
> *⁶ Don't worry about anything; instead, pray about everything. Tell God what you need, and thank him for all he has done.*
> *⁷ Then you will experience God's peace, which exceeds anything*

we can understand. His peace will guard your hearts and minds as you live in Christ Jesus. (Phil. 4:4, 6–7 NLT)

What does Paul first instruct the Philippian disciples to do? He tells them to rejoice in the Lord always. Paul knew the power of joy and rejoicing. Joy is not just a characteristic of kingdom life; it is a powerful spiritual force (Rom. 14:17). It was joy that gave Jesus the ability to endure the cross and suffering on behalf of all of humanity (Heb. 12:2).

Joy flows from your relationship with Christ, not from your external circumstances. Joy is an enduring spiritual reality of God's kingdom that will sustain you through challenging times. It is a characteristic entirely different from happiness. While happiness depends on "happenings" and can be fleeting when circumstances change, peace and joy flow from your relationship with God. When you are truly abiding in Christ, His peace and joy remain constant.

Your ability to rejoice in all circumstances safeguards your faith. God is always good, but suffering is part of your Christian walk. Difficult events happen in life, and many times you have no control over them. However, you do have control over how you react. God works everything for your good. Maintaining a right perspective during suffering will keep you in a place of peace. You can live full of God's joy despite hardships and setbacks.

Paul modeled the importance of always rejoicing in the Lord, even in difficult circumstances. In Acts 16, Paul and Silas were wrongly imprisoned in Philippi. At midnight, they chose to praise God during this terrible situation. Despite their hardship, their worship and joy in Christ positioned them for a miracle. God sent an earthquake that shook the prison, broke everyone's chains, and opened the prison doors. They were delivered, and the Philippian jailor and his household came to Jesus that night.

Later, in Paul's letter to the Philippian Christians, he encouraged them to rejoice in Christ. *"Whatever happens, my dear brothers and sisters, rejoice in the Lord. I never get tired of telling you these things, and I do it to safeguard your faith."* (Phil 3:1 NLT) His words are just as true for us today. Whatever happens, rejoice in the Lord. Never lose your praise and never lose hope. It may be midnight, but God specializes in the unexpected!

Paul learned that he could be content despite his circumstances (Phil. 4:11–12). He found real joy by focusing all his attention and energy on knowing Christ (Phil. 3:8) and obeying Him (Phil. 3:12–13). Real joy is in your union with Jesus—abiding in His presence daily. As Psalm 16:11 says, *"In Your presence is fullness of joy."* Your circumstances are not the problem; it is your perception of them that is the problem. Keep your focus on Jesus and let the joy of the Lord be your strength (Neh. 8:10).

Winston Churchill, former prime minister of England during WWII, said this, "if you are going through hell, keep going!" Keep your eyes and trust on Jesus; He will help you through the most difficult of circumstances. Your perception of circumstances defines whether you can overcome challenges. God is the Lord of breakthrough. When it looked the worst for England, God answered the prayer of His people. A nation and the world were eventually freed of evil tyranny as the allied forces landed in Normandy, France on D-Day.

The more you are in love with Jesus, the easier it is to rejoice always. When Jesus is your closest friend, His joy will have no limitations in your life. Genuine faith knows that God holds everything in His hands. You are His beloved, and He has your best interest in mind. A close relationship with Jesus will keep you in His peace, free of worry and fear. Trust Him continually and learn to rejoice in Him always.

Keep in mind that you are a citizen of heaven and ambassador of another world (See Phil. 3:10). Society and the world are your mission but not your permanent home. You have an eternal home and eternal purpose; earth is your temporary residence. You have a heavenly inheritance presently and in the future. You can rejoice because resurrection life is yours—now!

After Paul told the Philippians to rejoice always, he instructed them to pray always and not to worry. Prayer promises to bring us into a place of rest and God's peace. We are to give thanks in everything, not only when the difficult circumstances are over. Paul instructs us to tell God what we need and then to give thanks. We are to give thanks to God from a place of expectation, knowing that we have asked (*aitéo*), and we know that the answer is on the way. Gratitude keeps the heart postured in faith and God's peace. Confident prayer is thankful prayer, and it silences the thoughts of worry and fear.

You can't control the outcome of prayer, but you can control how you respond to the situation. Choose to remain in God's love, peace, and joy. Jesus lived in response to the Father, not in response to the devil or circumstances. Jesus modeled dependency on the Father and the Holy Spirit, He invites us to do the same. When we allow worry and fear to control us, we limit our authority as citizens of heaven. God wants you to ask and expect that He will answer. Worry and fear dilute your confidence that you have the right to petition God.

Jesus stripped the devil of his authority and delegated His authority to us (Matt. 28:18–20). However, the devil regains authority through our unbelief and agreement with his lies and schemes. When you worry, you empower fear and agree with the lies of the enemy. It opens the door to oppression and even depression.

Worry is a manifestation of unbelief or underdeveloped faith. The writer of Proverbs had something to say about worry, *"Anxiety (worry) in the heart of man causes depression, but a good word makes it glad."* (Prov. 12:25) Anxiety or worry can lead to discouragement and depression. One of the antidotes is to rejoice always as you confidently remain in Christ and his word. (In my book, *Fulfill Your Dreams*, I discuss in detail how to overcome worry and fear in a chapter titled *Worry Free Living*).

God wants you to be confident in petitionary prayer. But remember, prayer is primarily your intimacy and communion with God. You rest in Him through prayer, releasing worry and receiving His peace. Paul gave this admonition in his Philippian letter:

> *[8] And now, dear brothers and sisters, one final thing. Fix your thoughts on what is true, and honorable, and right, and pure, and lovely, and admirable. Think about things that are excellent and worthy of praise. [9] Keep putting into practice all you learned and received from me—everything you heard from me and saw me doing. Then the God of peace will be with you.* (Phil 4:8–9 NLT)

You must adjust your thinking to heaven's perspective—which is life giving and positive. Get rid of negative thinking and begin to refocus on positive thoughts and behavior. You will ward off worry and fear and be confident in your relationship with God. Prayer will become more confident, and you will have greater boldness to cry out to God.

You have the right to ask and God is expecting you do so! Pray with a demand on heaven, expecting God to answer, and cover your prayers with thanksgiving. Rejoice in God always and His peace and joy will keep you strong.

Chapter Nine

Elijah's Prayer Principles

"The prayer of the righteous person is powerful in what it can achieve." James 5:16 CEB

"The church has been negligent of one thing…She has not prayed the power of God out of heaven." John Lake

To live the abundant and victorious life Jesus intends, you must become a person of prayer and pursue communion with God. Faith is a prerequisite to answered prayer. Despite contrary circumstances, persist in prayer—His peace and joy will fill you. Prayer, based upon the promises of God and flowing from a place of intimacy with Jesus, brings the power of heaven to earth. Mountains move. Lives are changed. God is glorified.

Prayer is Communion

Through our faith in Christ and new birth by the Holy Spirit, we have fellowship with God. One of the joys of any relationship is communication. Jesus modeled a daily prayer life with the Father that demonstrated how simple and meaningful our fellowship with God can be. For Jesus, prayer was more than just bringing requests to the Father; it was conversing with Him in a two-way dialogue. Prayer is foremost a conversation with God. Through prayer, we learn how to abide in God's presence and engage in a conversation with Him to bring heaven's agenda to earth. God loves to make His heart known. Effective prayer agrees with the revealed will and purpose of God.

The foundation for effective prayer is intimate relationship with Jesus. As you walk faithfully with Him, your trust in God and confidence in prayer grow. There are no short cuts to a deep relationship with God. You must be intentional about your spiritual growth, since your prayer life springs from this fellowship. The Holy Spirit will help you in this journey, but you must set aside time to cultivate your relationship with Jesus. Learning how to converse with God simply will yield tremendous dividends in your life.

From a place of intimate relationship with God, He will show you how and what to pray. When you pray from heaven's revelation, it brings that reality into earth's realm. As a believer, your union with Christ positions you in His resurrection authority and power. You are praying from His victory to realize heaven's desire here on earth.

As it is in Heaven

Through God's Word and prayer, you gain perspective and more clearly understand His will. Through divine union with

Jesus, you have unhindered access to heaven's promises and provision. Prayer offers a follower of Christ the potential to bring future realities into the present.

So, you might ask, "How do I pray?" As we've examined, in Luke 11:2–4, Jesus gave instructions to the disciples about how to pray, saying, *"When you pray, say: Our Father in heaven, Hallowed be Your name. Your kingdom come, Your will be done on earth as it is in heaven."* *As it is in heaven* is a phrase filled with spiritual truth and reality. When you pray according to the discovered will of God as revealed through His Word and prayer, you are praying from heaven's perspective. This empowers you to pray for God's kingdom to "come on earth, *as it is in heaven.*" You are praying the revealed will of God.

Confidence in prayer develops as you learn to pray according to God's promises and revealed will. I have discovered that I am the most faith-filled and confident when I "know" what and how God wants me to pray. As I then pray with a heart of love and humility according to His nature and revealed will, I have an inner knowing and assurance the answer is on its way.

Prayer from heaven's perspective empowers you to pray for God's kingdom to "come on earth, *as it is in heaven.*" God's kingdom, or God's dominion, brings His authority and peace to your earthly situations. Your position is with Christ in heavenly realms (Eph. 2:6). His domain is near, and you should expect answers to your prayers and situations to change. You are not praying to break through to heaven; you can be confident and expectant in God that, as you pray according to His revealed will, the answer is on the way. Your prayers are helping to bring the reality of heaven to earth, which is your assignment (Psalm 115:16).

In Jeremiah, we read about God's invitation to the Israelites to enter future hope and promise: *"Ask me and I will tell you remarkable secrets you do not know about things to come."* (Jer. 33:3 NLT) God knew His future intent for this wayward nation—one filled with hope. He invited them, and encourages you today, to ask for the secrets and mysteries that God alone discloses. He wants to unveil glimpses of the future to you, to empower you to pray effectively, and bring tomorrow's promises into "today" for you. Many promises are "now words" for you. However, faith, prayer, and obedience are required to see promises and dreams become reality.

Paul wrote, *"[18] I pray that the eyes of your heart may be enlightened, so that you may know what is the hope of His calling, what are the riches of the glory of His inheritance in the saints, [19] and what is the surpassing greatness of His power toward us who believe. These are in accordance with the working of the strength of His might."* (Eph. 1:18–19) As a follower of Christ, the surpassing greatness of God's power accompanies your life. Because you are in Christ, God Himself empowers your prayer life. This power is not human effort but the inner strength of His might!

Paul wrote many times of this power in Eph. 1:19, 6:10, Col. 1:11, and 1 Tim. 6:16. In these verses, the English word *power* is translated from the Greek word *krátos*. *Krátos* means "strength, manifested power, and dominion."[1] The word primarily signifies exerted strength and power shown effectively in a governing authority. *Krátos*, as used in these verses, primarily refers to God's kingdom power, dominion, and majesty as demonstrated through the resurrection of Jesus. You are enthroned with Jesus in His *krátos*: His dominion, authority, and resurrection power.

You are united with Christ, with both His life and His power. *"Glory to God, who is able to do far beyond all that we could ask or imagine by his power at work within us."* (Eph. 3:20 CEB) Where is the power at work?—within you!

Jesus said in the book of John, *"³⁸Anyone who believes in me may come and drink! For the Scriptures declare, 'Rivers of living water will flow from his heart.'" ³⁹ (When he said, "living water,",' he was speaking of the Spirit, who would be given to everyone believing in him...)."* (John 7:38-39 NLT) Through your union with Jesus, you are in Him and His power within you. Through the Holy Spirit, the same power God demonstrated when He raised Jesus from the grave resides in you. You have a "River of Life" flowing within—don't dam the river of God's presence!

This means that presently, you have resurrection power attached to your prayer life. What does resurrection mean? It means raising back to life things that look or act dead. God demonstrated this *"power toward us who believe"* first *"in Christ, when he raised him from the dead, and seated him at his right hand in the heavenly places."* (Eph. 1:19-20) The power in you is the same power God demonstrated when He raised Jesus out of the grave; it is His resurrection power!

Declare the Drought is Over!

A few years ago, the state of Arizona had a terrible drought. For nearly two years, the drought intensified, causing a serious shortage of rain both summers, which would have normally been our rainy seasons. Arizona, and my city of Tucson, needed rain desperately.

During the height of the drought, Carolyn and I decided to escape the summer heat for the day and travel the Catalina

Highway to the top of Mt. Lemmon. Beautiful and majestic, the Catalina Mountains lie to the north of Tucson and rise dramatically above the valley floor. The Catalina Mountain Highway provides a picturesque view for the city's inhabitants and winds its way through nearly thirty miles of switchback roads to the 9,000-foot summit of Mt. Lemmon, the highest peak in the Catalina range. From the top of Mt. Lemmon, you can view the eighty square-mile valley and the city of Tucson below.

After walking some of the mountain trails, we decided to sit on large boulders that overlook the city. The rocks are a beautiful place to rest, take in the view, and pray for the city. We have spent the day on Mt. Lemmon many times over the years, often ending our time in prayer for our city. However, this day was different. As we prayed, Carolyn said to me, "Bob, I believe the Holy Spirit says to 'declare that the drought is over.'" When she said that, I immediately knew in my heart that this was God's revealed will and that we were to pray in agreement, declaring over our city and state that the drought was over.

It just so happened, as divine coincidences so often do, that I was in the middle of a six-week teaching series on prayer at our church entitled *The Elijah Principle*. Using 1 Kings 18 and James 5:16 passages about Elijah as examples of effective prayer, I was teaching that we should expect our prayers to be effective and powerful when we pray according to God's revealed will.

Carolyn and I prayed and declared for a few minutes that the drought was over for the state of Arizona and the city of Tucson. We called forth rain, declaring clouds to form and for an abundance of rain to fall. At the time, the sky was bright blue with no clouds. Yet we had that sense that something was about to happen. Faith sees as reality what is unseen to natural sight.

The following Sunday, I continued my teaching series and shared with the congregation about how we prayed and declared the "drought was over" from the top of Mt. Lemmon. We encouraged the church to pray in the same manner. I found out a couple of days later that on that same Sunday, a pastor in Phoenix also taught from the 1 Kings 18 passage. Someone suggested that I listen to his sermon, and I was surprised to hear the parallels in our messages, including his declaration over Arizona, "The drought is over." God was moving.

Within the next few days, we received that summer's first substantial rain in Arizona. The remnants of a hurricane, which had become a tropical disturbance, made its way across Mexico and eventually impacted Tucson and Arizona with significant rainfall—record breaking in some areas! We rejoiced, thanked God, and kept declaring, "The drought is over!" Ten days later, a second tropical disturbance came through southern Arizona—more record rainfall—and the rain deficit for the entire year of 2014 in Tucson was eliminated with these two storms. The power of united, believing prayer!

Thrust onto the Scene

Every aspect of God's kingdom manifest here on earth—in people, churches, and life—is first conceived and birthed by prayer. As described in 1 Kings 18:41–46, Elijah exemplified this truth when, as directed by the Lord, he continued to pray until the promise was fulfilled, and rain covered the drought-stricken land of Israel. Effective prayer acts upon the Father's revealed will and intercedes until the promise manifests on earth.

Elijah is an interesting OT patriarch. Revered in Scripture and Jewish tradition as a great prophet, God sent Elijah to turn the nation of Israel's heart back to the true worship of Yahweh. Yet we know little about him other than the fact that he was from Tishbe in Gilead. Elijah appears suddenly in the narrative of 1 Kings 17, bursting on the scene in dramatic fashion: *"Now Elijah, who was from Tishbe in Gilead, told King Ahab, 'As surely as the* Lord, *the God of Israel, lives—the God I serve—there will be no dew or rain during the next few years until I give the word!'"* (1 Kings 17:1 NLT) God backed the word He gave through Elijah, and a severe drought affected Israel.

During that time, God's covenant with Israel had been violated by their apostasy. Under the perverse leadership of King Ahab and his wife Jezebel, Baal was worshiped throughout the northern kingdom as the god of rain and fertility. They believed Baal could control the seasons, the crops, and the land. The writer of Kings declared the severity of the situation due to Ahab's leadership: *"...Ahab did more to provoke the* Lord *God of Israel to anger than all the kings of Israel who were before him."* (1 Kings 16:33)

Elijah confronted Ahab, the false prophets, and an apostate nation. God sent fire and rain to confirm that He is God and that Elijah was His spokesperson. The heavens opened and a national revival began. Almost overnight, Elijah went from obscurity to notoriety as a great prophet in Israel.

Later, God escorted Elijah from earth to heaven in a flaming chariot (2 Kings 2:11), but his influence was not over. His name is mentioned many times in Scripture, even throughout the NT. When John the Baptist began his ministry as the prophetic forerunner to Jesus, people asked him, "*Are you Elijah?*" and he answered, "*No.*" (John 1:21) Regarding John, Jesus said, "*And if you are willing to receive it, he is Elijah who is to come.*" (Matt. 11:14) Later, Moses and Elijah appear on the Mount of Transfiguration to talk with Jesus before His crucifixion and redemption of humanity (Matt. 17:1–13).

Elijah, as a renowned prophet in both Jewish and Christian tradition, continues to hold a special place within these communities and in the heart of God. His relationship with God and his earnest prayer for rain (1 Kings 18: 41–45) provide key principles for effective prayer—the type of prayer that prevails.

The Elijah Principle

In his letter to the twelve tribes dispersed throughout the Greco-Roman world, James used Elijah as an example for righteous living and faith-filled prayer. James, the half-brother of Jesus, was the first century apostolic leader of the church in Jerusalem. Church tradition attributes his namesake epistle to him. His letter provides practical instruction for believers to live virtuously and victoriously.

An interesting side note is that James was an unbeliever during Jesus' earthly ministry. However, according to Paul in 1 Corinthians 15:7, Jesus appeared to James after the resurrection and this most likely led to his conversion. The radiance of Christ softens even the hardened hearts of His biggest skeptics. Never quit praying for your family and friends, because Jesus loves them!

James states that righteous living and earnestness in prayer are principles to an effective prayer life:

> ¹⁶ *The earnest prayer of a righteous person has great power and produces wonderful results.* ¹⁷ *Elijah was as human as we are, and yet when he prayed earnestly that no rain would fall, none fell for three and a half years!* ¹⁸ *Then, when he prayed again, the sky sent down rain, and the earth began to yield its crops.* (James 5:16–18 NLT)

The English word *earnestly* is translated from the Greek word *energéō*. The word means to "act" or to "work."[2] However, it is not primarily human effort—it is spiritual. The implication is that God's Spirit is at work on our behalf.

The Amplified version of James 5:16b reads, *"The earnest (heartfelt, continued) prayer of a righteous man makes tremendous power available [dynamic in its working]."* (AMPC) The basic idea in the Greek is that prayer has energy. This energy, or power, is available to and through the followers of Christ by the Holy Spirit (Eph. 3:20; Jam. 5:16b). Your prayers, energized by the Spirit, are at work and cause things to change and manifest.

Notice how James compared Elijah to the ordinary reader of his letter in verse 17: *"Elijah was as human as we are..."* Elijah was revered as a great prophet in Israel, and early Jewish and non-Jewish readers alike would have known who Elijah was. James was stating a profound truth that Elijah was human, just like each of us; yet his prayer was effective because he was righteous, and he prayed sincerely.

James did not say, "Elijah, the great prophet, prayed and look at the results." Rather, he said (my paraphrase), "Elijah, an ordinary person like you and me, lived righteously and prayed with faith and zeal. God answered his prayers, and he will answer your prayers too."

I define *The Elijah Principle* as: "Earnest, sincere prayer by a righteous person, based upon the revealed will of God, when prayed with faith and expectation, is effective and powerful through the resurrection power of Christ and the Holy Spirit." In his pastoral letter, James was making a point to all believers that we can be effective in prayer like Elijah if we operate in similar prayer principles.

Elijah's Prayer Principles

Elijah received a word from the Lord: *"And it came to pass after many days that the word of the LORD came to Elijah, in the third year, saying, 'Go, present yourself to Ahab, and I will send rain on the earth.'"* (1 Kings 18:1) God revealed his will to Elijah, essentially telling him that He was going to send rain once Elijah confronted Ahab. Elijah was obedient to God's directive and confronted Ahab and the prophets of Baal. God backed up His prophet with fire from heaven upon the sacrifice, and all the people fell on their faces exclaiming, *"The Lord, He is God!"* (1 Kings 18:38–39) The false prophets were executed, and Elijah proclaimed to Ahab that he heard *"the sound of abundance of rain."* (1 Kings 18:41)

After Israel's heart turned back to God, the narrative continues with Elijah praying for rain (1 Kings 18:42–46). He was confident in what God had revealed. Elijah prophetically heard the sound of rain before a cloud was in the sky and prayed until the clouds formed and the rain fell. I would say this is effective prayer. Effective prayer is answered prayer!

Circumstances are subject to change when you operate according to God's revealed will and principles. God is sovereign, and He often acts apart from our involvement. Yet, even though He does not need to, God frequently chooses to partner with us to bring about His purposes on the earth. It is a mystery—God, the Creator, chooses to involve us in His purposes and the advancement of His kingdom.

Prayer has the power to transform circumstances for you and others. You might be just a prayer away from a dream becoming reality, a promise being fulfilled, or a miracle being performed. Let us look closely at the prayer strategy and principles of Elijah (1 Kings 18:42–46), which made his prayer effective and ended the drought.

Righteousness

Elijah prayed as a man in right relationship with God. Elijah was a human just like you and me—prone to weakness, discouragement, failure, temptation, and sin. However, James says that Elijah was righteous and that the *"prayers of a righteous person are effective."* Does this mean that everything Elijah did was perfect and without fault? No, he was a human just like us. He made mistakes and was not without sin. However, Elijah endeavored to walk faithfully with God, and God answered his prayers.

You might be wondering, "How righteous do I have to be to pray effectively like Elijah?" Paul wrote in 1 Corinthians 1:30 that *"Christ made us right with God; he made us pure and holy, and he freed us from sin."* (NLT) Jesus has become your righteousness, holiness, and sanctification. This means that through Jesus, God sees you presently as pure, holy, and in right standing with Him. You are an adopted son or daughter, united with Christ and His holiness, and because of that you pray in right relationship with God. You can approach His presence free of shame and condemnation, knowing that the Father's heart is for you, not against you.

However, while you are righteous through the blood of Christ, Scripture also exhorts you to live a holy life and to pursue righteous living (2 Cor. 7:1). Pursuing a blameless lifestyle removes potential hindrances to prayer. For example, Peter exhorted husbands to love and respect their wives: *"Treat her as you should so your prayers will not be hindered."* (1 Pet. 3:7 NLT) The writer of Psalms stated, *"If I regard wickedness in my heart, the Lord will not hear."* (Psalm 66:18 NASB, Prov. 6:16–19) The Bible warns of the necessity to live righteously, ensuring our prayers are unhindered.

In other words, In Christ, you are righteous, but you must pursue a righteous life. If you fall short in any area of your life, be quick to repent, ask God for forgiveness, and expect His cleansing (1 John 1:9). You are righteous through what Jesus did for us on the cross—live in His righteousness. Allow the Holy Spirit to make you more Christ-like each day (Rom. 8:29).

Elijah was human like us, but he learned to live in right relationship with God. Half-hearted obedience produces weak prayer. It causes you to lose confidence and robs your faith, hindering the power of the Holy Spirit in your life. God grants grace to the humble, not the proud. You can expect answers to your prayers if you are living a life that is committed and obedient to God, like Elijah. If you do not waver between two positions and live righteously, God will answer your sincere prayers in His timing.

Confidence in the Will of God
Elijah prayed according to the will of God (1 Kings 18:1). God's word revealed His will to Elijah: God promised him that after

he confronted Ahab, He would send the rain. Elijah could confidently obey the directive and pray in faith, knowing he was praying the revealed will of God. God keeps His promises; it's part of His unchangeable nature. He is not fickle or moody, and He never lies. He watches over His word to perform it. His word is His bond. Therefore, when we pray God's revealed will and word, we can trust that our prayers will be answered.

How do you know what to pray for? This may seem over simplistic, but you know what to pray for by hearing from God. Faith is a revelation to the heart, which begins with a word from God. The more specific your prayers are the more effective they will be. God does not answer vague prayers—pray with specificity.

Some of you may doubt your ability to hear God's voice. Jesus said, *"My sheep hear My voice, and I know them, and they follow Me."* (John 10:27) As a follower of Christ, you are part of God's sheepfold, and Jesus says that you can hear His voice. God may speak through the scriptures, through impressions, through the voice of the Spirit, through pictures and visions, through circumstances, and through other people. Learn to be sensitive and aware of His presence while you are in worship, prayer, and reading his Word. A verse may seem highlighted to you. You may get a strong impression about something or a mental picture. Someone may approach you and say something that seems odd but confirming.

There is a unique language in the Spirit by which God communicates to each of us. While God's language with all of us may have shared characteristics, you must learn to recognize how God communicates with you. If you are new to communing with God, be confident that you too can "hear" God's voice and know His will. As you pursue God, you will grow in your ability to discern His voice and learn to pray more effectively. However, keep in mind that any revelation, dream, or vision should agree with the tenor of Scripture and the character of God.

In addition, the Bible is full of promises that reveal God's will. In fact, there are nearly 7,500 promises recorded. Learning what promises are applicable for you today is important. Not all these promises are universal, as some are for unique situations and person(s) at a specific time. An example of a non-universal promise would be God's instruction to Joshua to take the city of Jericho—it was a specific promise to Joshua and the children of Israel (Jos. 6:3–5).

In Philippians 4, Paul gives an unconditional universal promise regarding provision: *"My God will meet your every need out of his riches in the glory that is found in Christ Jesus."* (Phil. 4:19 CEB) Unlike the promise to Joshua, the Philippian promise is applicable for us today. You should memorize this one—God will meet your every need!

Some universal promises are conditional, while others are not. For example, 1 John 1:9 begins, *"If we confess our sins..."*—conditional. Matthew 21:22 says, *"And whatever things you ask in prayer, believing* (conditional*), you will receive."* Psalm 66:18 says, *"If I regard iniquity in my heart* (conditional*), the Lord will not hear."*

However, an unconditional universal promise would be Psalm 119:105 which says, *"Your Word is a lamp for my feet."* This is always true, no matter what. Similarly, Titus 2:11 says that God's grace always offers salvation to everyone, unconditionally. Learning God's revealed will through the universal promises in Scripture, both conditional and unconditional, are critical for establishing a powerful prayer life.

The most effective prayer relies upon knowing God's will, which will give you faith to believe for it. If you are not sure of God's will, however, your prayers may waver and be less effective. James says, *"⁶ Whoever asks shouldn't hesitate. They should ask in faith, without doubting. Whoever doubts is like the surf of the sea, tossed and turned by the wind. ⁷ People like that should never imagine that they will receive anything from the Lord."* (Jam. 1:6–7 CEB) Sometimes our prayers are misguided, filled with soulish desires, and not from the Spirit. Greater clarity about the will of God creates greater faith for answered prayer.

Confidence in prayer develops as you learn to pray according to God's promises and revealed will. John wrote of this truth, *"¹⁴ This is the confidence that we have in our relationship with God: If we ask for anything in agreement with his will, he listens to us. ¹⁵ If we know that he listens to whatever we ask, we know that we have received what we asked from him."* (1 John 5:14–15 CEB) John emphasizes the confidence we can have from knowing God's will. He claims that confidence begins with our relationship with God. Prayer is foremost a dialogue with God—not just bringing petitions to Him. God desires relationship with you. Seek Him first, not the answers to your problems. If you only seek answers, often you will not find them; but if you seek God foremost, the answers will find you.

Provided that you are praying in full accordance with God's will, you can be confident that you have what you prayed for. The use of the present tense "we have" in 1 John 5:15 does not necessarily indicate an immediate manifestation of the thing you prayed for, but it does indicate an immediate assurance that the thing is already granted to you by God. It may take a while for its actual manifestation, but time cannot affect this initial assurance. Now, you can pray through the process until the desired result manifests.

I have discovered that I am my most faith-filled and confident self when I know what and how God wants me to pray. Mark 11:24 says, *"Therefore I say to you, whatever you pray and ask for, believe that you will receive it, and it will be so for you."* (CEB) A more correct translation would be that we have "already received" it. In the same way, 1 John 5:14-15 could be summed up as: "If you know that you are praying for anything according to God's will, you know that He hears you. If you know God hears you, you know that you have the thing you prayed for (this does not necessarily indicate immediate fulfillment)." From a faith perspective, receiving comes at the very moment of praying. After that, the actual manifestation of that which you have already received follows, according to God's timing.

How long do you pray? Continue to pray through an issue until you see one of three things happen: the manifestation of the answer to prayer, a sense of release by the Spirit to discontinue prayer, or your spirit begins to "praise through." Sometimes the Spirit will lead you to give God thanks and praise for the answer, even though it has not yet manifested. I've experienced this on more than one occasion. As the Holy Spirit gave assurance of the answer, I simply began to thank and praise God—before seeing the manifestation in the natural. Once this happens, the natural manifestation often occurs quickly!

God's promises reveal what His will is, but prayer brings the fulfillment of what God has promised. Elijah prayed with zeal and confidence because he had a clear revelation of the will of God. The greater understanding you have regarding the will of God, the more effective your prayers will be.

Persistence

Because he knew God's will, Elijah prayed with persistence. Bowed down with his face between his knees, reminiscent of an ancient eastern birthing position, Elijah persisted in prayer until clouds formed and rain fell. To persist in prayer requires humility, obedience, and faith in the revealed will of God.

Elijah persisted in prayer seven times before the cloud formed and the rain began. What if he had quit praying after just six times? He had to persist in prayer until the Spirit gave him a sense of release. It is easy to give up on dreams, promises, and miracles. Like a slow leak, our faith can ebb over time, leading us to lose hope and quit praying. Jesus said, *"Men always ought to pray and not lose heart."* (Luke 18:1)

Keep in mind that miracles are the result of prayers either by you or for you. I have wondered what types of prayers were prayed over our church property in the 1950's. Is it possible that some of what Passion Church is experiencing today is a result of another generation's prayers? Absolutely. Persistence is vital to realizing the fulfillment of prayer.

Paul wrote to the church in Galatia, *"My little children, for whom I labor in birth again until Christ is formed in you."* (Gal. 4:19) The metaphor Paul used here indicates persistence in prayer—like a woman giving birth—that continued until the nature of Christ was formed in them. The persistence Paul described is like Elijah's prayer for rain. God created us to persist. We discover who we are and how great God is during challenges and adversity. Your obstacle is an opportunity to persist in prayer.

God is bigger than your biggest problem or biggest dream. Do not bring God down to your level of understanding. Rather, pray from His eternal perspective and maintain a "high view," not a "low view" of God. One of the reasons many give up too soon in prayer is that they make a wrong assumption—the answer has not come, so we must have failed. In truth, we only fail when we quit praying. Our reach must be greater than our ability to grasp.

What do you do when others have their prayers answered, but yours seem to go unanswered? Do not let offense toward God take root in your heart. Focus on what God is doing and persist in prayer. Many of your prayers will take time to materialize. Keep in mind that when God seems to be saying "no," it might be a "not yet." His timing is always best.

George Muller was a nineteenth century minister who cared for over ten thousand orphans in his lifetime and relied solely upon God through prayer for provision. He recorded in his journal that he prayed for five of his friends to accept Christ. After many months, one of them came to the Lord. Ten years later, two others were converted. Twenty-five years passed before the fourth man was saved. Muller persevered in prayer for his fifth friend for fifty-two years, until the time of his death. He never gave up believing that his friend would accept Jesus. After Muller's funeral, his last friend came to Christ. God rewarded his faith and persistence—but Muller did not see the full answer to his prayer on this side of eternity.

Jesus told an interesting parable in Luke 11:5–8 about prayer and persistence. A man knocked on his neighbor's door at midnight to borrow some bread. At first, he was told to go away, "I am in bed and so is all the family." However, the man kept on knocking, until most likely everyone in the house was awake, including the animals. Because he continued knocking, the man opened the door and gave him the bread. Jesus said that the reason he got up and opened the door was not because it was the right thing to do, but because of his neighbor's persistence. In the Luke 11:5–8 passage, the Greek word used for persistence is *anaideia* and is a strong word meaning "shameless persistence." *Anaideia,* or shameless persistence, describes a person who will not take no for an answer.[3]

This parable is found in the first part of Luke 11, which is all about prayer. The disciples have asked Jesus to teach them how to pray, and He gave them the Lord's Prayer as a model. Immediately following, He shares this parable in verses 5–8. Jesus then gives a threefold admonition:

> [9] *And so I tell you, keep on asking, and you will receive what you ask for. Keep on seeking, and you will find. Keep on knocking, and the door will be opened to you.* [10] *For everyone who asks, receives. Everyone who seeks, finds. And to everyone who knocks, the door will be opened.* (Luke 11:9–10 NLT)

Jesus encourages His disciples to continue to ask, seek, and knock—with a shameless persistence—until the door is opened or the answer is realized.

Depending on the circumstance, God may require that we persist in prayer. In Genesis 32, Jacob wrestled with an angel, or as many scholars believe Jacob may have wrestled with God

Himself. They wrestled all night, and even though his hip was put out of joint, Jacob said, *"I will not let you go unless you bless me."* (Gen. 32:26) He would not let go of God until God blessed Him—a shameless persistence. God honored his request and blessed him.

In Mark 7:24–30, a Gentile woman begged Jesus to cast a demon out of her daughter. *"No,"* Jesus said, *"it is not fair to take the children's food and throw it to the dogs."* Yet despite the insult, she would not let Him go. She replied, *"Even the dogs under the table eat the children's crumbs."* Moved by her faith and persistence, Jesus cured her daughter and exclaimed, *"Good answer! Now go home, for the demon has left your daughter."* (Mark 7:29 NLT)

In Mark 2, four men carried their paralyzed friend to Jesus. The crowd was so dense they could not get near Him. Desperate for a miracle, they removed the roof of the house and lowered the man to Jesus—that is persistence! Jesus healed their friend and he walked home.

One of the ways persistence manifests is in your ability to wait upon the Lord. Isaiah describes a persistent waiting, *"Yet those who wait for the LORD will gain new strength…"* (Isa. 40:31 NASB). I believe Elijah could pray with power and persistence because he knew what God's will was and he learned how to abide in God.

Persistent prayer is not about knocking on the door of God's heart until He eventually answers your prayer. Rather, persistent prayer reflects a deep desire, passion, and confidence in God, and therefore is honored throughout the Bible. This type of prayer often comes from a place of great love for God and desire for others to know Him.

Faith

As we examined in the early chapters, faith is important as you pray. Faith is an assurance that God has answered your prayer. Elijah believed his prayer was answered even before the answer came (1 Kings 18:44–45). God revealed His will to him, and Elijah obeyed by meeting with Ahab (1 Kings 18:1). Elijah could pray confidently because he had faith for the miracle. Elijah had the assurance that rain would come (1 John 5:14–15).

Faith is substantive. It is the assurance of the answer even while it is not yet fully in sight. When the eyes of your heart believe God's will for a situation, you have the reality of the answer even though it has not yet manifested. You persist, even if it seems like God is distant, because you know the Lord hears. Psalm 34:7 states, *"The righteous cry out, and the Lord hears."* You pray from your identity as a child of God, accepted and heard by your loving Father.

In the parable of the unjust judge and the widow, God promises to answer our requests quickly (Luke 18:1–8). But then Jesus asked this question at the end of the parable, *"Nevertheless, when the Son of Man comes, will He really find faith on the earth?"* We are to pray in faith, knowing God is just. Jesus emphasized the importance of having faith that perseveres.

We persist and do not give up because we are children of a just God. We pray in faith, believing that *"God exists and that he rewards those who sincerely seek him."* (Heb.11:6 NLT) If faith fails, then prayer stops. Who continues to pray when they lose faith? Faith inspires prayer, and the act of prayer strengthens our faith. If I want more faith, I must look to Jesus, who is the author and finisher of my faith. Faith provides eyes to the heart to see what God is offering.

Faith operates from the invisible realm to the visible realm. Faith is not a condition of the mind, but a divinely imparted grace to the heart. Faith comes from God. As you learn to wait on Him, He deposits more faith in your heart. Great faith is rarely developed in a moment, though it is a gift from God. Your faith grows as you obey Him and exercise the measure of faith He has already given you.

Faith understands God's authority and the power of His promises. The Roman Centurion in Matthew 8 exhibited this type of faith when he requested Jesus heal his servant by simply speaking a word. Jesus marveled at the man's faith, and He *"said to those who followed, 'Assuredly, I say to you, I have not found such great faith, not even in Israel!'"* (Matt. 8:10) *Faith*, from the Greek *pístis*, is a forward-leaning assurance of the answer because of confidence in the one who's granting the desired petition.[4]

Faith is not an intellectual understanding, but rather it springs from a revelation in your heart by the grace of God. As such, it is an imparted grace given to you by Christ. Whether it is a promise from God's word, or an inspired word from the Spirit, faith builds through the word revealed. I once heard it said, "Well-developed faith is often tied to well-developed prayers." Prayer, combined with strong faith, pulls the unseen reality of God's promises into our world.

Jesus only did what He saw the Father do (John 5:14). Everything that Jesus did, including putting mud on the blind man's eye, was rooted in His ability to discern and know the Father's will. His discernment enabled Him to see and to understand the revealed will of God. Your new life in Christ empowers you to see God's purposes with spiritual eyes.

Perhaps it seems like the heavens are silent and God is distant. During those times, remember to pray from a place of sonship, knowing your identity. As a child of God, you are related to a loving Father who knows your every need before you ask or think of it. Pray knowing your identity is in Christ. Pray from a place of trust in the finished work of Jesus. Pray knowing that God's Spirit indwells you, and that your prayers are more than mere human words.

Prayers are like prophecies, with the power to transform the direction of your life. Your prayers have creative power within them. Job says, *"Declare a thing and it shall be established."* (Job 22:28) Prayers of faith and the decrees of heaven have the power to move mountains before you. Learn to declare on earth *as it is in heaven.* George Muller said, "Faith does not operate in the realm of the possible. There is no glory for God in that which is humanly possible. Faith begins where man's power ends."

Faith is an expectant anticipation of a promised outcome. Do not despise the day of small beginnings. At first, Elijah only saw a small cloud in the distance before it grew into a downpour. James wrote, *"In the same way, faith is dead when it doesn't result in faithful activity."* (Jam. 2:17 CEB) Elijah prayed confidently for a miracle because he had faith in the One making the promise. Are you in a challenging situation currently? Are you standing confidently upon God's promises?

Normal People, Full of Faith, Impact Nations
With the eyes of faith, Elijah was assured of what God was about to do, and his faith led him to act. Several years ago, while I was preparing for an evening service on a mission trip

to Brazil, God spoke a very poignant word to me. I was preparing to lead a team to minister and we were expecting that God would pour out His Spirit to touch and heal the people.

God said to me, "If you see yourself as merely human, you will function as merely human. However, if you see yourself as a supernatural being, empowered by my Spirit, then you will function as a supernatural being." This word impacted me. I had fresh confidence that God would work through us.

It was a powerful meeting. Nearly everyone we prayed for either said that their pain left, significantly improved, or were completely healed. Elijah, who was just a man, prayed and God answered. How much more effective should our prayers be under the New Covenant, since the Holy Spirit now dwells within us?

Your mission is to bring resurrection life to situations that need reviving. Both the Bible and church history record the stories of ordinary men and women who have allowed God to use them powerfully. Courageous faith and fullness of the Spirit are required to claim great exploits in His name (Dan. 11:32b). Elijah could not produce rain as a mere human, yet James 5:17–18 tells us that his prayers did. Your prayers have the weight of heaven behind them. Droughts cease and situations change when prayed according to God's will and pattern.

When your life is completely surrendered to Jesus and your motivation is to do only what you see the Father doing, then God can use you in remarkable ways—even to impact a nation. You can look on things that are dead and declare life. Effective prayer brings heaven to earth. It releases God's power and makes it possible to change the course of history. You are a prayer away from the release of the power of His resurrection life into situations you face. Pray!

Chapter Ten

Our Eyes are On You

"O Lord God of our fathers, are You not God in heaven, and do You not rule over all the kingdoms of the nations, and in Your hand is there not power and might, so that no one is able to withstand You?" 2 Chr. 20:6

"Prevailing prayer is that which gets an answer." Charles Finney

Do you believe in miracles? I do. When I'm in the direst of circumstances, my faith rests in *El Shaddai*—God Almighty. God is a God of miracles. He is the same yesterday, today, and forever. I love to read Bible accounts, church history, and hear testimonies of God miraculously intervening for His people. These accounts testify of God's faithfulness and invite us to believe He will do it again.

Recently someone shared a powerful testimony with me that reveals the power of prevailing prayer and God's miraculous intervention. Anita detailed how the Lord woke her at 3:00 a.m. one morning to pray for a senior level manager's daughter. She didn't know the man personally, but God gave her a specific word to deliver to him that day. She said to God, "I can't just go into the office of a senior level manager and tell him I have a message from God!" She continued in prayer until about 5:30 a.m. for the man and his daughter.

On her way to work, still concerned about giving this man God's message, the Lord simply said to her, "I'll bring him to you today!" Anita responded, "Deal!" Later, she was in a 9:00 a.m. training class, when this manager, who wasn't scheduled for the training, arrived for the class. During the break, he approached Anita and asked if he could speak with her privately.

Anita took her moment to tell him what God revealed in the early morning hours, "Don't lose faith; continue to fight in prayer for your daughter. Stand in the gap for her life." After hearing God's word, the man broke down in tears because no one knew anything about his daughter's heart condition, which was a result of Leukemia. Don't you love the faithfulness of God! The story gets better. A short time later, the man shared with Anita how his daughter was completely healed! God is a God of miracles, but He often chooses to use us as part of the process, and it is with faith-filled, prevailing prayer.

There are moments in our lives when it seems all of hell is raging against us. And perhaps hell is. Circumstances may seem insurmountable, and the oppression overwhelming. Jesus promised us abundant life, but the enemy comes to take what is rightfully ours, "*The thief does not come except to steal, and to kill, and to destroy. I have come that they may have life, and that they may have it more abundantly."* (John 10:10) When sickness and disease rob us of vitality, when financial hardship leaves us fearful, when relationships are fractured with no hope of restoration, we must pray in faith knowing that miracles never cease.

There's a wonderful story of the miraculous deliverance of God's people in 2 Chronicles 20:1-30. The narrative begins with a desperate situation:

> *[1] It happened after this that the people of Moab with the people of Ammon, and others with them besides the Ammonites, came to battle against Jehoshaphat. [2] Then some came and told Jehoshaphat, saying, "A great multitude is coming against you from beyond the sea, from Syria; and they are in Hazazon Tamar" (which is En Gedi).* (2 Chr. 20:1-2)

King Jehoshaphat and the children of Judah were surrounded by enemies. Historians estimate they were outnumbered 60 to 1. It appeared to be an impossible situation to overcome. But as they prayed and sought the Lord for strategy, God revealed to them what to do. Ultimately, God supernaturally defeated their enemies and gave them deliverance and victory—without going to war! Their warfare was spiritual. They prayed, worshipped and obeyed God's directives. The battle belonged to God.

Jehoshaphat started his reign at a young age. He was a righteous king who revered the Lord. During his time in power, he removed the high places and groves in God's land used for idol worship. He sent his army into these places and tore them down (2 Chr. 18). He was zealous for God and determined to bring the nation back to true worship and righteous living.

Jehoshaphat's righteous actions demonstrate an important principle for us to replicate individually and corporately. We too should remove old areas of our lives not dedicated to the Lord. When we are born again through the cross of Christ, we become the very righteousness of Christ, and He becomes our sanctification (1 Cor. 1:30). But Paul also admonishes us to pursue righteous living and holiness (2 Cor. 7:1). We are to live as a new creation in Christ (Col. 3:1–11).

However, Jehoshaphat didn't stop there. Having torn down the high places, he sent teachers to teach the principles of the Word of God. It's not enough to simply remove the negative aspects of our lives—we must rebuild our lives on the Word. We must replace the empty places in our lives with the truth of God's Word and the presence of His Spirit. The more God's Word is a part of you, the more you can live from the divine reality of your union with Christ and the Holy Spirit. In the process, faith grows, and prayer strengthens.

The Enemy's Attack

After King Jehoshaphat removed the idolatrous high places and rededicated them to the Lord, the enemy surrounded Jehoshaphat and the people of Judah, ready to attack and destroy them. As I mentioned, when this overwhelming enemy army came upon them, it seemed like a hopeless situation.

Here is a key principle: when God moves in our lives, individually or corporately, the enemy attempts to stop us from advancing the kingdom of God. The moment you or your loved ones take back territory from the enemy, the thief then comes to steal, kill, and destroy (John 10:10). Who should the devil attack? A lukewarm Christian? Perhaps, but most often the enemy targets those who are close to the Lord, and those who are moving in His power to reach the lost and hurting of our world. Which churches does the enemy attack? He attacks the ones with a kingdom vision, moving in God's love and power, because they are a threat to the enemy's kingdom!

> *³ And Jehoshaphat feared, and set himself to seek the Lord, and proclaimed a fast throughout all Judah. ⁴ So Judah gathered together to ask help from the Lord; and from all the cities of Judah they came to seek the Lord.* (2 Chr. 20:3–4)

Notice Jehoshaphat's initial reaction: he feared! It's easy to become fearful when the situation looks hopeless. The COVID-19 pandemic in 2020 is causing havoc. The nations are reeling; people are fearful of death and economic calamity. Fear has gripped much of the world. The enemy intends to inflict human suffering and death to stop the advancement of God's kingdom. However, like Jehoshaphat and the children of Judah, as we pray, worship, and obey the Lord and His appointed leaders, we can be assured that God will fight the powers of darkness arrayed against us and we will see a victory.

My encouragement to you is to act responsibly while trusting God's Word. Psalm 91 tells us not to fear when dire circumstances surround us:

> *⁵ You shall not be afraid of the terror by night, Nor of the arrow that flies by day, ⁶ Nor of the pestilence that walks in darkness, Nor of the destruction that lays waste at noonday…⁹ Because*

you have made the LORD, *who is my refuge, Even the Most High, your dwelling place,* ¹⁰ *No evil shall befall you, Nor shall any plague come near your dwelling;* (Psalm 91:5-6; 9-10)

Because you have made the Lord your refuge, you do not have to fear the enemy's assault. Rather, you can rest in God's protection and care, trusting Him always.

Jehoshaphat allowed fear to propel him to action. He and the people began to fast and pray, and God began to move. After prayer, one of the prophets proclaimed:

¹⁵ And he said, "Listen, all you of Judah and you inhabitants of Jerusalem, and you, King Jehoshaphat! Thus says the LORD *to you: 'Do not be afraid nor dismayed because of this great multitude, for the battle is not yours, but God's.* (2 Chr. 20:15)

Did you catch this: Do not be afraid! Why? The battle is God's! We pray for governmental, scientific, and economic leaders to have divine wisdom and direction to stop COVID-19. We believe in science and the medical community. We adhere to proper hygiene and pandemic practice. We support their efforts. But, as a faith community, we know ultimately it is God Who will bring the breakthrough. He fights our battles and stops our enemies. He is *El-Shaddai*— God Almighty!

Have you ever felt "outnumbered 60 to 1?" I know I have. Perhaps world events or your current circumstance has caused you to fear. Fear is the opposite of and counterfeit to faith. When we look at challenging circumstances from a natural perspective, hopelessness overtakes us. When we function from our new life in Christ, the Spirit empowers us to act upon God's promises—despite the fearful circumstances we face.

Despite his initial fear, Jehoshaphat turned his fear to warfare: he sought the Lord with prayer and fasting in the land. He now leads the nation to act and prays:

> *⁵ Then Jehoshaphat stood in the assembly of Judah and Jerusalem, in the house of the Lord, before the new court, ⁶ and said: "O Lord God of our fathers, are You not God in heaven, and do You not rule over all the kingdoms of the nations, and in Your hand is there not power and might, so that no one is able to withstand You?*
>
> *⁷ Are You not our God, who drove out the inhabitants of this land before Your people Israel, and gave it to the descendants of Abraham Your friend forever? ⁸ And they dwell in it, and have built You a sanctuary in it for Your name, saying, ⁹'If disaster comes upon us—sword, judgment, pestilence, or famine—we will stand before this temple and in Your presence (for Your name is in this temple), and cry out to You in our affliction, and You will hear and save.'*
>
> *¹⁰ And now, here are the people of Ammon, Moab, and Mount Seir—whom You would not let Israel invade when they came out of the land of Egypt, but they turned from them and did not destroy them— ¹¹ here they are, rewarding us by coming to throw us out of Your possession which You have given us to inherit. ¹² O our God, will You not judge them? For we have no power against this great multitude that is coming against us; nor do we know what to do, but our eyes are upon You.* (2 Chr. 20:5–12)

Out of this prayer, three prayer principles emerge. We pray based upon who God is, what God has done, and what God has said.

We Pray Because of Who God Is

First, we pray based on who God is. Jehoshaphat begins his prayer not with a petition, but by praising God Himself and His character. If you begin with your need, your focus is wrong. Prayer isn't reminding God how serious the situation is. God almighty, the one who knows our sitting down and rising, knows our every need. Therefore, we must cultivate a relationship with God to really know who He is, what He is like, and what His character demonstrates.

Jehoshaphat turns his eyes away from the armies surrounding them. He refuses to listen to the voice of fear running through his mind. Instead, he fills his heart and mind with the greatness of God, *"O Lord God of our fathers, are You not God in heaven, and do You not rule over all the kingdoms of the nations, and in Your hand is there not power and might, so that no one is able to withstand You?"* (2 Chr. 20:6)

The Great Recession and a New Sanctuary

Do you remember the financial crash of 2008? It led to what economists have termed "The Great Recession," which was the largest economic downturn our generation has ever experienced. The housing bubble burst, unemployment soared, the stock market plummeted, and the banking industry stalled. Many feared an economic apocalypse. Amid this chaos, God impressed upon the leaders of our church and I to proceed with building a new church sanctuary. God's timing is not always our timing. Advancement and security can be opposites.

In early 2007, I began to work with an architect and officials from the city and county to move a street easement in our vacant lot. We could not build a new sanctuary without this step. Everything was on track to complete the easement change by late summer 2008. During the same period, I had several conversations with the vice president of our bank regarding a construction loan. Like the easement, the initial work toward a loan went smoothly.

In early September 2008, the city, county, and church signed the paperwork to move the easement. The city and county officials joked with me, "We think this is a first for the city and county to work so efficiently together on a project like this!" We all had a good laugh, and I left the city planning building that morning thanking God for answered prayer and giving us favor with the government. Little did I know that a horrific financial storm was brewing in our nation.

The ink was barely dry on the easement papers when the crash hit. Like most Americans, I was in shock. In a moment, everything had changed for our nation and our new sanctuary project. The odds of getting our construction loan were now stacked against us. I called our banker, who said politely, "Bob, no one is lending money right now. We honestly have no idea when we are going to be able to lend funds for construction or mortgages. I'm truly sorry." You could say we were "outnumbered on every side." But we continued to worship, pray, and believe for God's sanctuary to be built during a challenging season.

In mid-January 2009 as I prayer walked around the church property, God said to me, "Bob, I want the new church sanctuary built." I did not hear an audible voice but a firm impression from the Holy Spirit to my spirit. The impression to construct the new building was strong, and yet my mind found several reasons why it was not a good idea to start. News headlines declared economic turmoil in the country. The stock market was still in a free-fall, with no bottom in view. In the natural, it did not make sense. After more prayer, we determined that God *was* directing us to build this new sanctuary—despite the recession. God specializes in moving obstacles during the most challenging seasons.

Every lending institution I called for a construction loan said, "I'm sorry, we are not lending now." We kept praying, and I kept calling. God wanted His sanctuary built. Finally, the Lord led me to a company in Michigan who was willing to fund our church construction project through the sale of bonds. The catch was that over a million dollars in bonds needed to sell to fund the project. We were optimistic and convinced the bonds would sell. They did, but not in our timing.

We started the construction project in late 2009, taking a step of faith and clearing our vacant lots. By the spring of 2010, enough of the bonds sold to pour a concrete foundation for the new building. As bonds sold, construction continued. The walls of the new building were slowly emerging. The timing of the project was predicated on the completion of bond sales by the summer of 2010. Unfortunately, by that date only about seventy percent of the bonds had sold. The contractor could no longer build without complete funding. The project came to a grinding halt in late 2010.

At that time, I went for a hike in the mountains near Tucson and asked God for wisdom and direction. The remainder of the bonds needed to be sold and additional funds raised in order to complete the project. A partially constructed building was not a completed sanctuary. To relieve stress, I hiked quickly, crying out to God in prayer.

Suddenly, I saw a vision the Lord had given me when He first directed us to build the new sanctuary. I saw Jesus building a stone wall in a row of beautiful Ponderosa Pines! He was wearing a leather apron and looked rugged and dirty from the demanding work. He was happy and determined to finish the task. Jesus was taking stones and securing them onto the wall with mortar. He had all the strings and measuring sticks needed to ensure the wall was straight. Then He paused, turned to me and said, "Bob, I want my building built." When the Spirit renewed this assignment to me, new faith rose within me to complete the construction. I kept hiking and praying—my faith was beginning to go to new heights.

I remembered the opposition Nehemiah faced with his building project. The enemy attempted to stop him from God's appointed assignment. With God's help, Nehemiah and his team finished the wall around Jerusalem in remarkable time. There never is a "right time" to advance God's kingdom or undertake His projects, there will always be opposition. There is only God's timing, and it requires a persistent faith to press on despite the challenges. We are to fight the good fight of faith and stand firm in who God is, what God has done, and what God has promised.

We continued to pray and sell bonds, as we entered 2011 with hope to finish the project. Then, another setback hit. One afternoon, just when construction began to progress again, the contractor called and said, "Pastor Bob, I'm sorry. I need to quit the church sanctuary project. I'm going out of business."

I was in shock and angered over the situation. The contractor had not been forthright about the project, but at the same time, the slow bond sales contributed to some of his problems. He, like many contractors during that time, ended up filing for bankruptcy. Our building was only about seventy percent complete and we had just lost our contractor. Once again, we found ourselves praying and reminding God of who He is and what He had promised us.

The church board found another contractor. The new contractor quickly assessed the progress of the project and gave us a proposal to complete the building. The remaining bonds had to sell, and we needed another three hundred thousand dollars. That may not seem like a lot considering the scale of church building projects, but it was a large amount for our congregation, especially during a recession. Miraculously, God helped us complete the project by selling the remaining bonds, raising donations, and borrowing short-term funds from private individuals.

We worked with the new contractor in a timely fashion to finish the sanctuary by December. Our first service in the new building was Sunday, Christmas Day, 2011. Jesus had His building built! Within two years, we refinanced the church mortgage and repaid all remaining short-term loans. When God guides, He provides, and orchestrates all the pieces into beautiful harmony. Whatever the situation may be, God can bring the right people and the right provision into place at the right time. It's who He is.

We Pray Because of What God Has Done

Jehoshaphat is standing in the land that God has promised them, and declares, *"Are You not our God, who drove out the inhabitants of this land before Your people Israel, and gave it to the descendants of Abraham Your friend forever?"* (2 Chr. 20:7) Jehoshaphat reminds God of His covenant with Abraham and how God drove out the inhabitants of the land before the descendants of Israel. It was sovereign and supernatural.

To paraphrase, Jehoshaphat declared in prayer, "God, you drove out the inhabitants of this land and gave it to us as the inheritance you promised. We were descendants of slaves, an unorganized people, but God you supernaturally moved every obstacle because it was your will and purpose to give us this land. Now Lord, if we are going to stay here, it will be by your supernatural hand!"

He is essentially saying, "God you did something supernatural back then as we focused our eyes on you. Now Lord, you are the One who helped us cross the Red Sea and the Jordan, placing our feet on this land as you promised! Now Lord, move again to keep us in this land!"

Jehoshaphat recalls the testimony of God's power bringing the children of Israel into the promised land. He asks God to do it once again. By praying a testimony, he is reminding God, "Your testimonies are an invitation for you to do it again!"

God spoke to Moses regarding signs He would perform before Pharaoh, *"If they will not believe you or heed the voice or the testimony of the first sign, they may believe the voice or the witness of the second sign."* (Exodus 4:8 AMPC) Voice or testimony here means "a loud sound, voice, or call."[1] Testimonies *call aloud* the good works of God. Testimonies have their own voice and they declare loudly what God has done. Testimonies are an invitation to future miracles.

The Psalmist declares,

> *⁵ For He established a testimony in Jacob, and appointed a law in Israel, which He commanded our fathers, that they should make them known to their children; ⁶ That the generation to come might know them, the children who would be born, that they may arise and declare them to their children, ⁷ That they may set their hope in God, And not forget the works of God, But keep His commandments...* (Psalm 78:5–7)

The testimonies established in Israel call aloud the greatness of God to future generations. Jehoshaphat understood this. Testimonies compel others to place their faith and trust in God and not forget His mighty acts. The testimonies of God's mighty acts, nature, and character build faith in our children, and future generations. When we remind each other of what God has done, our confidence grows, and prayer is energized.

John connects testimony with the revelation of Jesus, *"... for the testimony of Jesus is the Spirit of prophecy."* (Rev. 19:10) Testimony is translated from the Greek word *martyria* and means, "witness: through firsthand knowledge or testimony: the content of what a witness tells."[2] A testimony is the spoken or written record of anything God has done in history. In this verse, the testimonies bear witness to the work of Christ.

Paul wrote, *"our testimony among you was believed."* (2 Thess. 1:10) In other words, Paul and others not only proclaimed the testimony of Christ but bore witness to the power of these truths. The Thessalonians believed God's witnesses and their message. Testimony has power associated with it—to save, heal, and deliver!

Testimonies can be prophetic in nature. Prophecy either foretells (declares future events) or forth tells (causes a change in the present). When Jehoshaphat declared the testimony of God bringing the children of Israel into the Promised Land, he was prophetically "forth telling" what God was about to do again. Faith was connected to his prayer; it became a prophetic declaration inviting God's miracle power to intervene once again for God's people.

There are healings and miracles, and then there are extraordinary miracles. In Acts 19, we read, *"God did extraordinary miracles through Paul."* (Acts 19:11) God was performing unusual miracles through Paul near Ephesus, and these miracles became widely known. They were the type of miracles that caused people to reflect upon Christ and the gospel message—much like when Jesus turned water into wine (John 2:1–12). Miracles glorify God and point to the reality of His kingdom among humanity.

A Notable Miracle

One of the most notable miracles observed at Passion Church involved a woman who came to our food pantry ministry one day. She came seeking bread but left with something much greater.

Routinely, volunteers in this ministry ask people if they would like prayer, specifically for healing. My wife, Carolyn, and another lady at our church asked this woman if she would like prayer. She said yes but did not specify why exactly she needed prayer. Despite this, the ladies began to pray for her. Not long into the prayer, one of the intercessors had an impression that there was something wrong with the woman's feet.

The woman was astonished they knew she had a problem with her feet. As the ladies continued to pray for her, all the pain in her feet left—she was healed! The woman was startled by her healing but excited about what God had done for her.

As a result of her healing, the woman asked the ladies to pray for her kidneys. She explained to them that she was on dialysis because one of her kidneys was not functioning and the other was functioning only at thirty percent. Carolyn said a short, commanding prayer for the kidneys to be restored and to function normally in Jesus' name. The woman thanked them for praying for her, took her food, and left.

Two months later, the woman returned to the church for another box of food. As she was leaving, she said to one of the volunteers, "Oh, by the way, I went to the doctor after the ladies prayed for my kidneys two months ago. The doctor was amazed."

At her next doctor's exam following the prayer, the doctor asked her what kind of treatment she received for her kidneys. The woman replied, "None. I had the people at the church pray for me." The doctor responded, "Well, it is a miracle, because both of your kidneys are functioning one-hundred percent!" The woman claimed that the doctor wrote an article about her miracle kidney healing. We were never able to get a copy of the article, but we continued to see the woman return to the church in good health for some time after.

I have shared this testimony several times over the years and have subsequently observed others receive healings from kidney disorders. God is a healer, and He still works miracles today. Jesus is the same yesterday, today, and forever. While critics and skeptics argue whether miracles ever happened or still happen today, the poor in Spirit, who are rich in faith, are still witnessing the healing and miraculous power of Jesus. Declaring a testimony is a vehicle by which the prophetic promise can be transmitted to others in need.

The gospel is prophecy, for it declares the testimony of Jesus. Every time the good news is proclaimed, it is an invitation for others to respond to the power of the testimony and be saved by God's power. *"Jesus Christ is the same yesterday, today and forever!"* (Heb 13:8)

The testimonies of the Lord are our inheritance. The Psalmist declares, *"I have inherited Your testimonies forever, for they are the joy of my heart."* (Psalm 119:111 NASB) A testimony is the written or spoken record of anything God has done in history—for others or for you. Can you remember a time when God helped you? Do you have any history of restoration with God? Pray with the confidence of what He has done for you and others in the past. Testimony-based prayer is an invitation to the miraculous!

We Pray Because of What God Has Said

King Jehoshaphat prayed based on who God is, what God has done, and finally based on what God has said.

It's a good thing Jehoshaphat knew what God had said. If he didn't know what God promised, he wouldn't have prayed confidently with God's Word. If he had not prayed in this way, the enemy would have stolen their inheritance! When we pray according to God's revealed will and promises, we can be confident that our requests are heard and will be answered. God watches over His Word to accomplish it.

What does this look like? It may look like a confident prayer over finances, "God you said we are to seek you first, your kingdom, and your righteousness and you then promise to meet our needs. Father I'm standing on your covenant promises to provide!" Or it may be a declaration of God's healing power, "Father, you said 'by His stripes we are healed.' So, Jesus, I thank you for healing that is available to me through your death and resurrection, and I ask for complete healing of my condition!"

When we know what God has promised, we can assertively pray with an expectation of the answer. God loves when you stand on His Word. The adversary trembles when Christians understand their authority in Christ and the power of praying God's promises.

Many believers receive their victory based on the sovereignty of God, but if they don't know about their God-given inheritance, the enemy will attempt to take from them their financial breakthrough, healing, or God-given destiny. Someone might say, "Well I guess it wasn't God's will, or I guess it was just my wishful thinking." No! Do you know what God has promised you? If you don't know what God has promised you—your rightful inheritance—you'll make no claim on it.

A few years ago, we had a water heater break in our sanctuary. Thankfully, it occurred early on a Monday morning. One of our staff members discovered the rising water in the foyer before the entire building was flooded. Carolyn and I received the "dreaded phone call" on the first day of a summer vacation. Our staff went into action calling a plumber, emergency reclamation company, and our insurance company.

It was a challenging situation. However, we had good insurance and what could have been thousands of dollars of expenses was covered almost entirely by our policy. We had a good understanding of what type of damage and repairs were covered, so making a claim on our "covenant policy" was easy! Know what God has promised you, and confidently pray His Word daily, not just when you're going through a storm. You will pray effectively when you need answers the most.

A pastor friend of mine recently shared this miracle testimony with me, "A woman came to our church with stage four lung cancer two weeks ago. She had all the air tubes hooked up to her and the doctors had given her ninety days to live. We prayed for her and she went to her oncologist. The report? Her cancer is completely gone from her body!" This is the power of Jesus working through believers who know what God has promised.

God has promised us in His Word—in His "covenant policy"—that healing is part of the work of Jesus on the cross. Healing is available *now* through the atoning work of Christ. Learning to fight the fight of faith through prayer and standing on what God has promised, whether for healing or any situation, is essential to living in victory. The woman received her miracle healing from stage four lung cancer because a church knew what God had promised and how to pray when surrounded by an enemy.

Jehoshaphat knew the enemy had no right. To paraphrase, he was making a bold declaration, "Right here Lord, it says in your covenant this land is ours forever! Therefore, enemy, you can try and send sixty to one against us, but God said it's our land forever. I'm putting my feet down on the solid rock of God's Word!" God's Word is full of many promises, hide His word in your heart, make your claim upon what He has promised, and stand firm. Sometimes a tenacious spirit is needed to claim God's promises. As Wigglesworth said, "God loves it when we make a demand on His Word!"

How do you pray when hell has broken loose against you?

First, go to God alone. If your eyes are on the great multitude coming against you, then you may become discouraged. When they are on God and His throne, all things become possible. The writer of Hebrews declares this truth, *"Therefore let us draw near with confidence to the throne of grace, so that we may receive mercy and find grace to help in time of need."* (Heb. 4:16 NASB)

Secondly, remind yourself what God has promised in His Word, beginning with Christ's victory. Jesus declared,

> *And I tell you, you are Peter [Greek, Petros—a large piece of rock], and on this rock [Greek, petra—a huge rock like Gibraltar] I will build My church, and the gates of Hades (the powers of the infernal region) shall not overpower it [or be strong to its detriment or hold out against it].* (Matt. 16:18 AMPC)

The powers of darkness have been defeated by the death and resurrection of Jesus. Learning to stand confidently upon His victory is essential to fighting the good fight of faith. The victory is now ours. In fact, the enemy's gates can't stop a confident believer and victorious Church.

Thirdly, make a demand based on who God is, what He has done, and what He has said. This is your key to victory! Remind yourself of the goodness of God, that He is with you always, and that He promises to be your ever-present help in times of need. He is El Shaddai, God Almighty, and nothing is impossible for Him. Remind yourself of God's miraculous testimonies throughout Church history. They are a prophetic invitation for God to do it again. Remind yourself of what God has promised in His Word and what the Spirit has spoken to your heart. Knowing the promises of God gives you a platform to stand firm against adversity.

Your Son Will be a Quadriplegic!
Recently, I attended one of our Life Groups on a Wednesday night, and heard this powerful testimony. Pete and Sandy were leading the Bible study and told a miracle story about their teenage son who was in a terrible auto accident twenty-two years ago. His car had flipped and his neck and back were severely injured. When Sandy arrived at the hospital, the doctors report was dire, "It's very bad, the x-rays show his neck has been broken and we need to get him into surgery right away; he will most likely be a quadriplegic."

Pete and Sandy were new Christians, who, in their words, "had one foot in the world and one with God. We weren't fully committed to Jesus yet." But they began to pray and committed themselves to follow God whole heartily. The hospital staff instructed them that their son would be in rehab for thirty days, and they needed to prepare their house for when he came home as a quadriplegic. But their son was confident, "No, I'll only be in rehab two weeks!"

The surgery went well, and their son said he could feel numbness in his right leg—a good sign. Once in rehab, to the shock of the staff, he began to regain movement quickly, and within ten days was released from rehab with normal motor functions! The only exception was slight loss of movement in his right hand. God worked a miracle! Even the doctors later said it was impossible, based on the x-rays, for their son not to be a quadriplegic!

Be Strong and Of Good Courage
What enemies are you facing today? Are your eyes on Jesus? Are you trusting in who He is, what He has done and what He has promised? Fill your heart and mind with God's Word and stories of His faithfulness. Refuse negativity and pessimism about God and His promises. Let your faith grow in a fertile heart that is free of doubt and unbelief. When you pray, pray with confidence that God hears your prayer and is ready to answer. Remember, it is God who calls those things that are not as though they are, and it is He who gives life to the dead and impossible situations!

Courageous faith is needed by God's people. Without Godly confidence, the believer is at risk to passively endure what the enemy brings. It may be less risky to withdraw and disengage in advancing God's kingdom, but Jesus calls us to something greater, to impact nations by His authority and power.

As His followers, we should be confident because we serve the resurrected King of Kings. We are united with Him in His ascension glory and authority and are partakers of His divine nature (Eph. 2:6; 2 Pet. 1:4). To walk in false humility—never using the authority we have been given through Christ's commission (Matt. 28:18–20), the authority of His name (John 16:23–24), or the empowering of the Holy Spirit (Acts 1:8)—does disservice to His victory. Simply stated, being falsely humble doesn't glorify Jesus. Genuine humility recognizes that apart from Jesus, "I can do nothing, but with Christ, all things are possible!"

As God encouraged Joshua, *"Have I not commanded you? Be strong and of good courage; do not be afraid, nor be dismayed, for the LORD your God is with you wherever you go,"* (Jos. 1:9) we need to be reminded that God intends His people to be strong and confident through Him. Learn to rely confidently on our Almighty God, knowing that He is always with you and will never leave you nor forsake you (Heb. 13:5).

Confident people, who walk humbly with their eyes set upon God, impact our world with His love and power. Although Elijah couldn't produce rain from his own strength his prayers led to breakthrough. Paul couldn't create new birth or maturity in the Galatians, yet Galatians 4:19 implies that his intercession did. We can't produce spiritual sons and daughters through human abilities, yet Isaiah 66:7-8 tells us that travail can. Be bold and confident as you pray. God will cause the enemy to flee before you, mountains to move, and bring the answers your heart desires!

Recently the Lord said to me during a Sunday service, *"I'm turning the bitter waters sweet!"* I picked up my Bible and turned to Exodus 15, where God told Moses to throw a tree into the bitter waters of Marah so the children of Israel could drink. As he did, the waters were made sweet so the people could drink (Exodus 15:22-27).

As I pondered this word, I sensed God telling me to encourage the congregation to believe prayers are being answered. God will turn situations, which have been bitter and challenging, into sweet waters. He is Jehovah Rapha, the Lord our Healer (Ex. 15:26). He will heal, restore, and make all things new—trust Him. It's through faith and patience that we inherit His promises. Stand firm and continue in faith and prayer, your answer is on the way!

Acknowledgements

Thank you to all my friends and colleagues at Global Awakening—you've made theology and ministry exciting and meaningful! Thank you, Steve Greene and Charisma Media—grateful for all you do! Thank you, Passion Church family and leaders who have believed in and supported me, as their pastor the past 18 years. I want to thank Glenn Wristen, Jason Anderson, Karen Pierson, Danielle Baethge, Hannah Goswick, Samuel Anderson, Charis Anderson, and my wife Carolyn for being such a great church staff. You have helped shoulder the load enabling me to teach, speak, and write—thank you. I am also grateful to Madeline Henners for your editing of the final manuscript. Thanks to Trevor Crosby for the cover portrait photo. Thanks to Jenny Chandler and the team at Elite Authors for the cover design and book layout. Thank you to the many who prayed for me as I wrote this book—Jane Quijada, Karen Pierson, Diana Bramlett, and Elise Arnold in particular. A special thank you to Carolyn for your prayers, love, and support—you enable me to wear many hats!

About the Author

In 2002, Dr. Bob and Carolyn Sawvelle established Passion Church in Tucson, Arizona. Prior to coming to Tucson, they served as missionaries in Haiti and as youth and missions pastors in Florida. Over the years, they have made numerous short-term ministry outreaches to Belize, Brazil, Guatemala, Haiti, India, Israel, Mexico, Mozambique, Romania, Tanzania, Ukraine and Venezuela.

In 1994, while on a stateside trip from Haiti, they were powerfully touched by the Holy Spirit in meetings at Catch the Fire Toronto, and then again in 1995 during meetings with Dr. Randy Clark in Melbourne, Florida. Since that time, they have desired nothing less than to be filled with God's presence and to allow His love and power to flow through them to change and heal the lives of others. Bob has a heart for the poor and hurting, and he believes that God is wanting His people to carry God's love and power beyond the four walls of the church buildings to those in need. Bob has a passion to teach and equip the body of Christ to operate in the fullness of the gospel of the kingdom.

Bob and Carolyn have been trained in healing ministry through Global Awakening Ministries and the Catch the Fire

Ministries. Additionally, they have received training in prophetic ministry from Christian International Ministries and Global Awakening Ministries. They both are ordained ministers. Bob has a D.Min. and M.Th. degrees.

Bob has published three books, *A Case for Healing Today, Receive Your Miracle Now,* and *Fulfill Your Dreams.* Bob is a doctoral mentor at United Theological Seminary (UTS), working with leaders who are earning their Doctor of Ministry degrees with the Randy Clark Scholars group at UTS. Bob is an adjunct professor teaching master's level courses at the Global Awakening Theological Seminary (GATS). Bob also is a course facilitator with Global Awakening's online Christian Healing and Prophetic Certification (CHCP and CPCP) programs.

More written and video teachings from Bob can be found on his website bobsawvelle.com, passiontucson.org, and on his YouTube, Facebook, and Instagram pages (Bob Sawvelle). Bob also has a weekly podcast with Charisma Podcast Network (CPN) called *Empowered for Purpose*, and is available on iTunes, Google Play, Spotify and other platforms (more info on his website).

Endnotes

Chapter One

1 Johannes P. Louw and Eugene Albert Nida, *Greek-English Lexicon of the New Testament: Based on Semantic Domains* (New York: United Bible Societies, 1996), 425.

2 James Strong, *A Concise Dictionary of the Words in the Greek Testament and The Hebrew Bible* (Bellingham, WA: Logos Bible Software, 2009), 20.

Chapter Two

1 The boy's symptoms resemble those of epilepsy: he is seized and thrown down, foams at the mouth, grinds his teeth, and becomes rigid. This is not an indication that epilepsy is the result of demonic possession, but that demonic possession can sometimes be manifested in physical symptoms, sometimes manifestations that are painful and tormenting (Mk 1:26; 9:25; Luke 13:11). Demons can cause disease, but not all illness is caused by demonization—discernment is needed.

2 Johannes P. Louw and Eugene Albert Nida, *Greek-English Lexicon of the New Testament: Based on Semantic Domains* (New York: United Bible Societies, 1996), 375.

Chapter Three
1 Including women and children, some scholars estimate as many as 20,000 people were fed.
2 Barclay M. Newman Jr., *A Concise Greek-English Dictionary of the New Testament* (Stuttgart, Germany: Deutsche Bibelgesellschaft; United Bible Societies, 1993), 68.
3 Charles S. Price, *The Real Faith for Healing* (Gainesville, FL: Bridge-Logos Publishers, 1997), 9.

Chapter Four
1 Charles Spurgeon, *Morning by Morning*, (Old Tappan, NJ: Fleming H. Revell, 1984), 80, 295.
2 Price, *The Real Faith for Healing*, 46.
3 Ibid, 51.
4 Ibid, 76.
5 Paul L. King, *Only Believe*, (Tulsa, OK: Word & Spirit Press, 2008), 347.

Chapter Five
1 Henry George Liddell et al., *A Greek-English Lexicon* (Oxford: Clarendon Press, 1996), 1569.
2 Gerhard Kittel, Gerhard Friedrich, and Geoffrey William Bromiley, *Theological Dictionary of the New Testament* (Grand Rapids, MI: W.B. Eerdmans, 1985), 505.
3 Johannes P. Louw and Eugene Albert Nida, *Greek-English Lexicon of the New Testament: Based on Semantic Domains* (New York: United Bible Societies, 1996), 161.
4 Ibid, 375.
5 Ibid, 437.
6 James Swanson, *Dictionary of Biblical Languages with Semantic*

Domains: Greek (New Testament) (Oak Harbor: Logos Research Systems, Inc., 1997).

Chapter Six
1. Smith Wigglesworth, *Smith Wigglesworth on Healing* (New Kensington, PA: Whitaker House, 1999), 78.
2. William Arndt, Frederick W. Danker, and Walter Bauer, *A Greek-English Lexicon of the New Testament and Other Early Christian Literature* (Chicago: University of Chicago Press, 2000), 123.

Chapter Seven
1. St. Patrick, *The Confession of St. Patrick*, 16, https://www.ccel.org/ccel/patrick/confession.pdf, (accessed March, 2019).
2. Ibid, 19.
3. Ibid, 23.
4. https://www.britannica.com/biography/Saint-Patrick (accessed Mar 2019)
5. Ibid.
6. http://www.grandmaslittleblackbook.com/Saint_Patrick_Miracles.html (accessed Mar 2019)
7. E.M. Bounds, *Power Through Prayer* (New Kensington, PA: Whitaker House, 1982), 58.
8. Helarion Alfeyev, *The Spiritual World of Isaac the Syrian* (Kalamazoo, MI: Cisercian Publications, 2000), 77.
9. James Swanson, *Dictionary of Biblical Languages with Semantic Domains: Greek (New Testament)* (Oak Harbor: Logos Research Systems, Inc., 1997).
10. Haddon Robinson, *Jesus' Blueprint for Prayer* (Grand Rapids, MI: Discovery House Publishers, 2000), 20–21.

11 Ibid., 21.
12 https://www.merriam-webster.com/dictionary/litotes (accessed Mar 2019)

Chapter Eight
1 Kittel, G., Friedrich, G., & Bromiley, G. W. (1995). *Theological Dictionary of the New Testament* (581). Grand Rapids, MI: W.B. Eerdmans.
2 Oswald Chambers, *My Utmost for His Highest: Selections for the Year* (Grand Rapids, MI: Oswald Chambers Publications; Marshall Pickering, 1986), June 7.
3 Johan Lust, Erik Eynikel, and Katrin Hauspie, *A Greek-English Lexicon of the Septuagint: Revised Edition* (Deutsche Bibelgesellschaft: Stuttgart, 2003), αἰτέω.

Chapter Nine
1 Wilhelm Michaelis, "Κράτος (θεοκρατία), Κρατέω, Κραταιός, Κραταιόω, Κοσμοκράτωρ, Παντοκράτωρ," ed. Gerhard Kittel, Geoffrey W. Bromiley, and Gerhard Friedrich, *Theological Dictionary of the New Testament* (Grand Rapids, MI: Eerdmans, 1964–), 908.
2 Gerhard Kittel, Gerhard Friedrich, and Geoffrey William Bromiley, *Theological Dictionary of the New Testament* (Grand Rapids, MI: W.B. Eerdmans, 1985), 254.
3 Johannes P. Louw and Eugene Albert Nida, *Greek-English Lexicon of the New Testament: Based on Semantic Domains* (New York: United Bible Societies, 1996), 627.
4 Ibid., 375.

Chapter Ten
1 William Lee Holladay and Ludwig Köhler, *A Concise Hebrew and Aramaic Lexicon of the Old Testament* (Lciden: Brill, 2000), 315.
2 James Swanson, *Dictionary of Biblical Languages with Semantic Domains: Greek (New Testament)* (Oak Harbor: Logos Research Systems, Inc., 1997).

Made in the USA
Middletown, DE
07 January 2023